If I Were a Bird, You'd Be The First Person I'd Shit On

Swearing N' Coloring

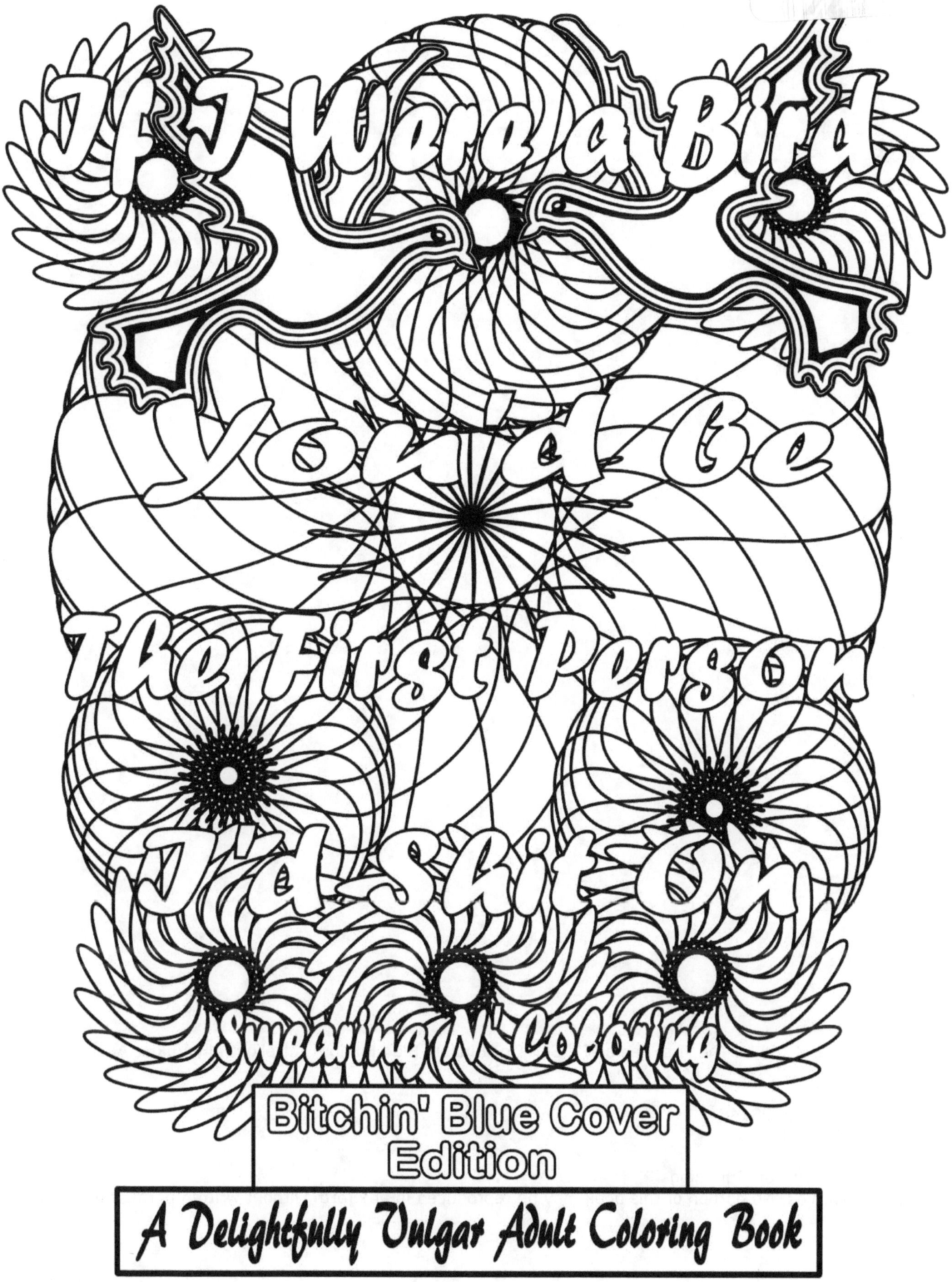

Bitchin' Blue Cover Edition

A Delightfully Vulgar Adult Coloring Book

If I Were a Bird, You'd be The First Person I'd Shit On: Bitchin' Blue Edition: A Delightfully Vulgar Adult Coloring Book

ISBN-13: 978-1533528148
ISBN-10: 1533528144

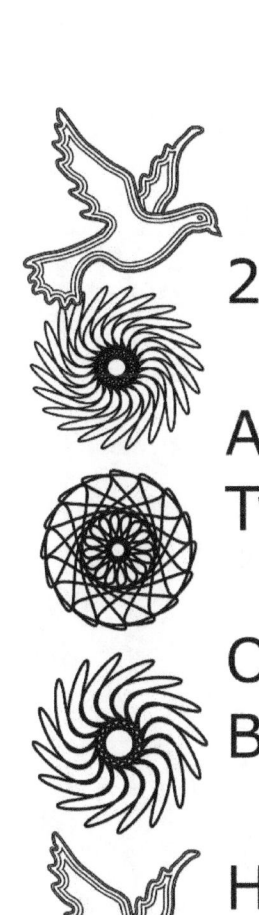

22 Unique Swear Word Designs.

All Illustrations Are Printed Twice!

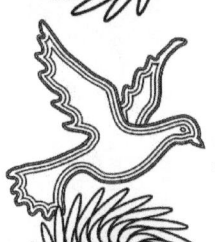
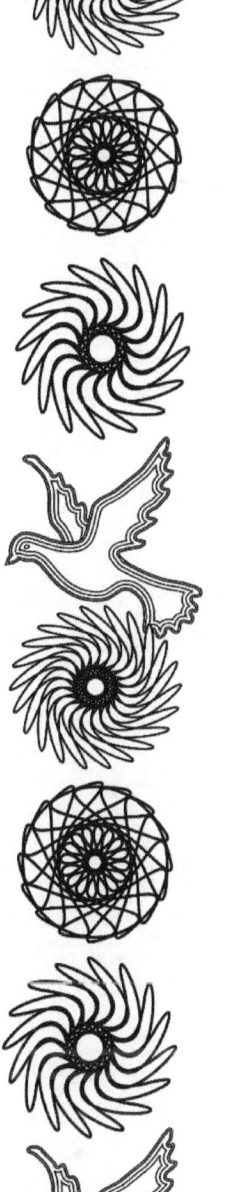

One-Sided Designs To Prevent Bleed-Through

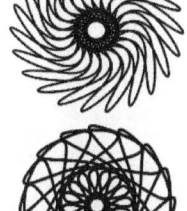

Hours Of Relaxation! Excellent Stress Relief!

Use Your Own Coloring Tools. Crayons, Colored Pencils, Or Markers!

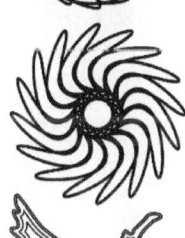
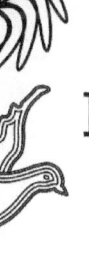

Start Fucking Coloring Today!

It's The Shit!!!

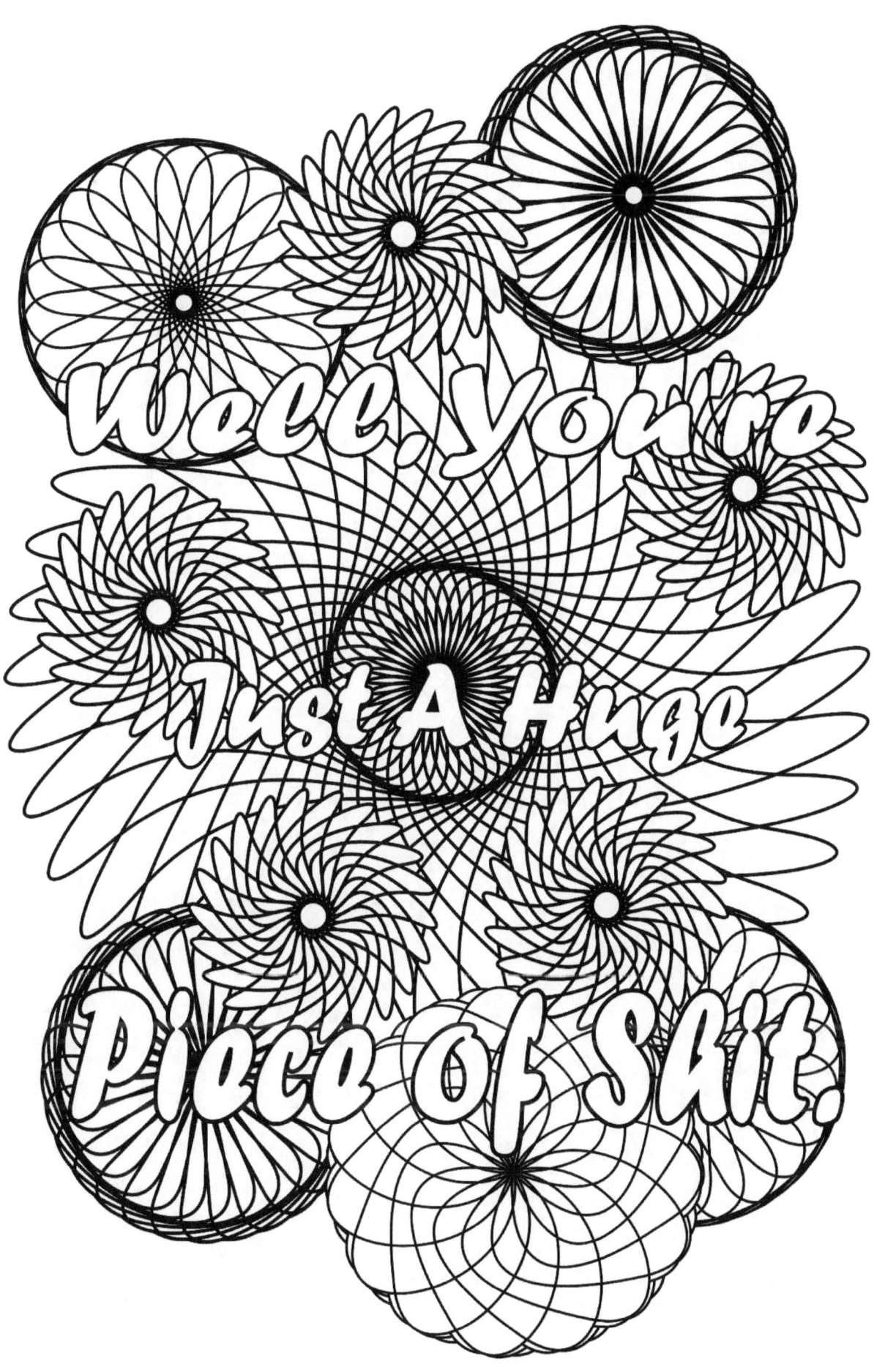

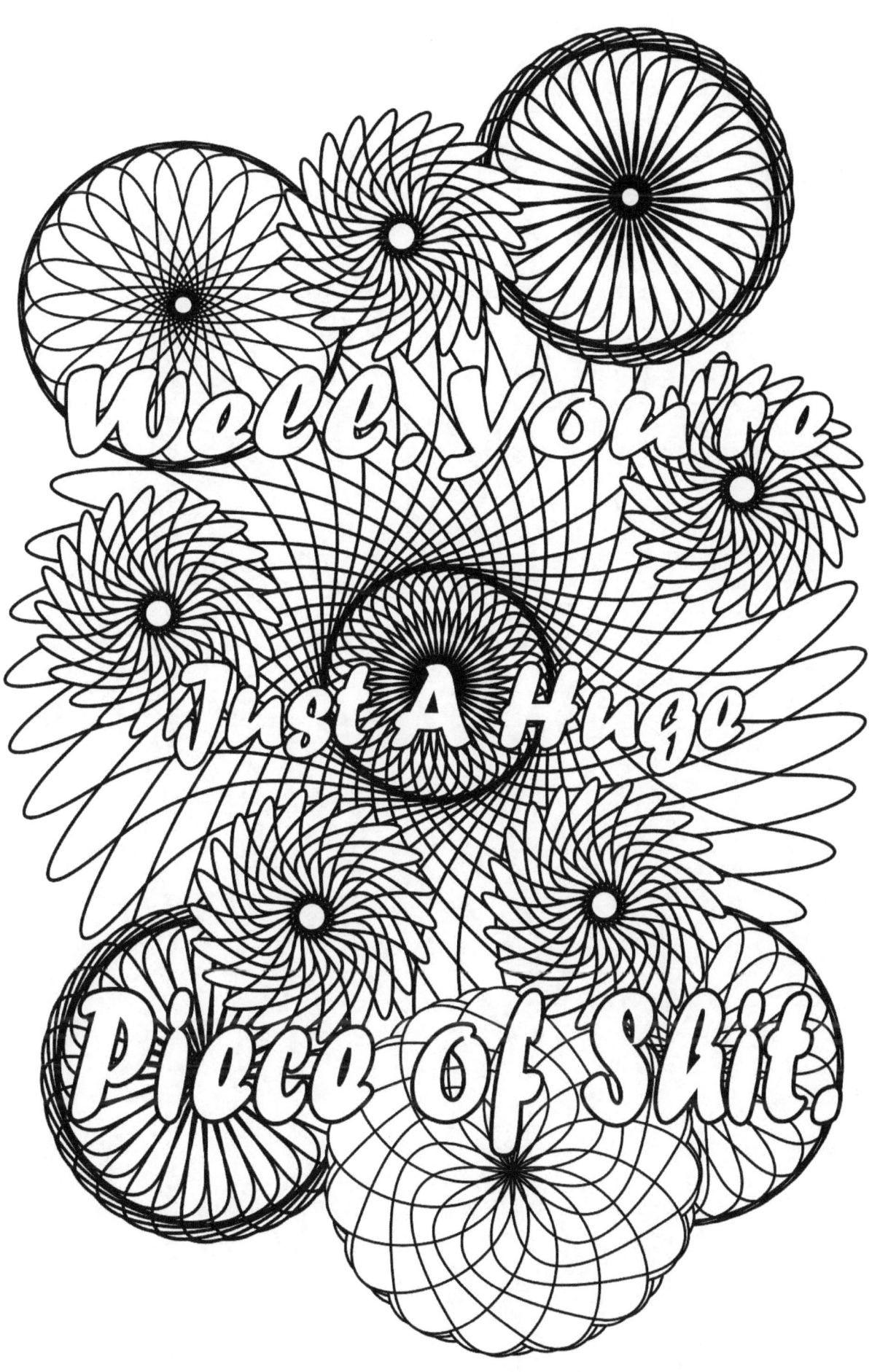

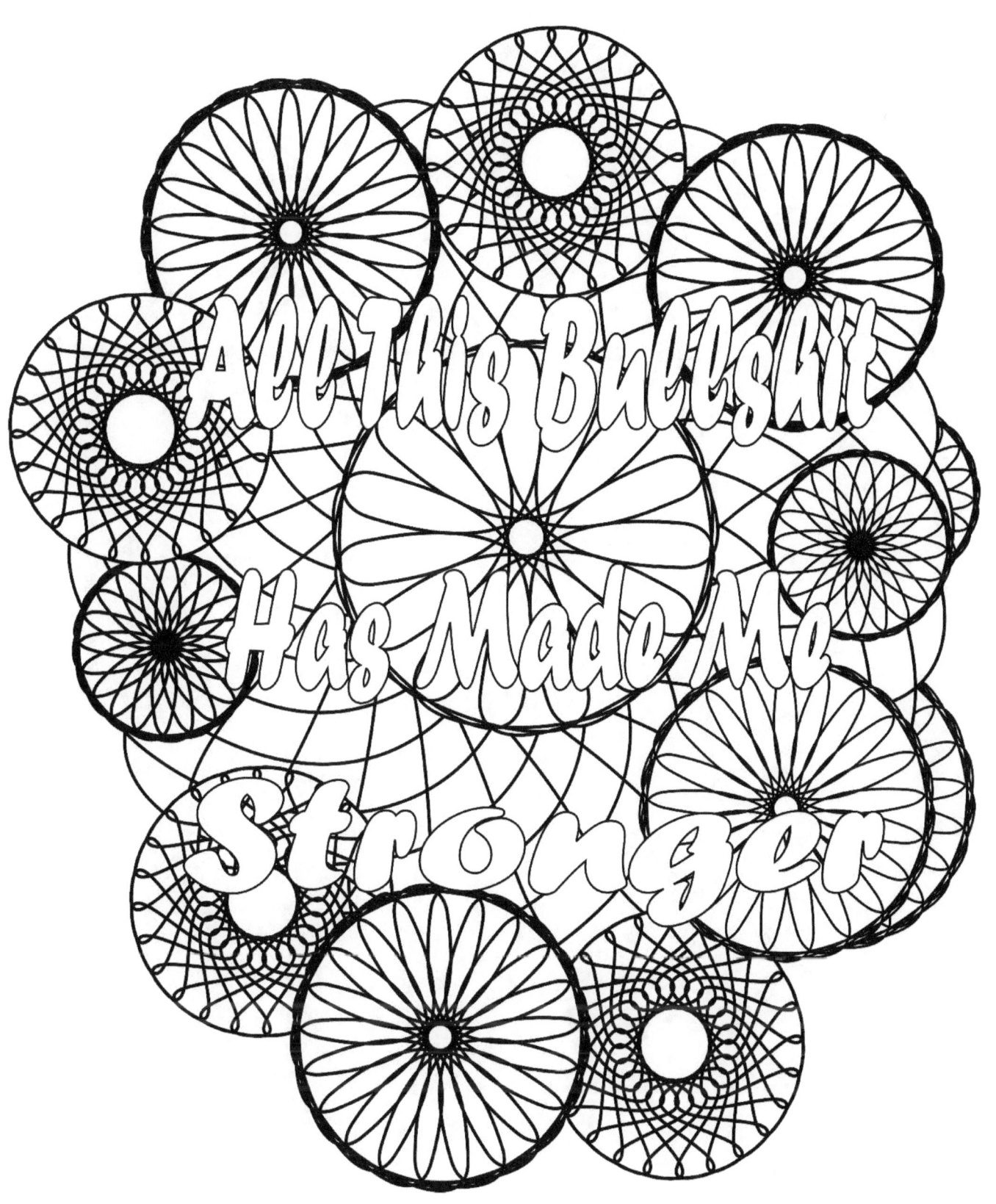

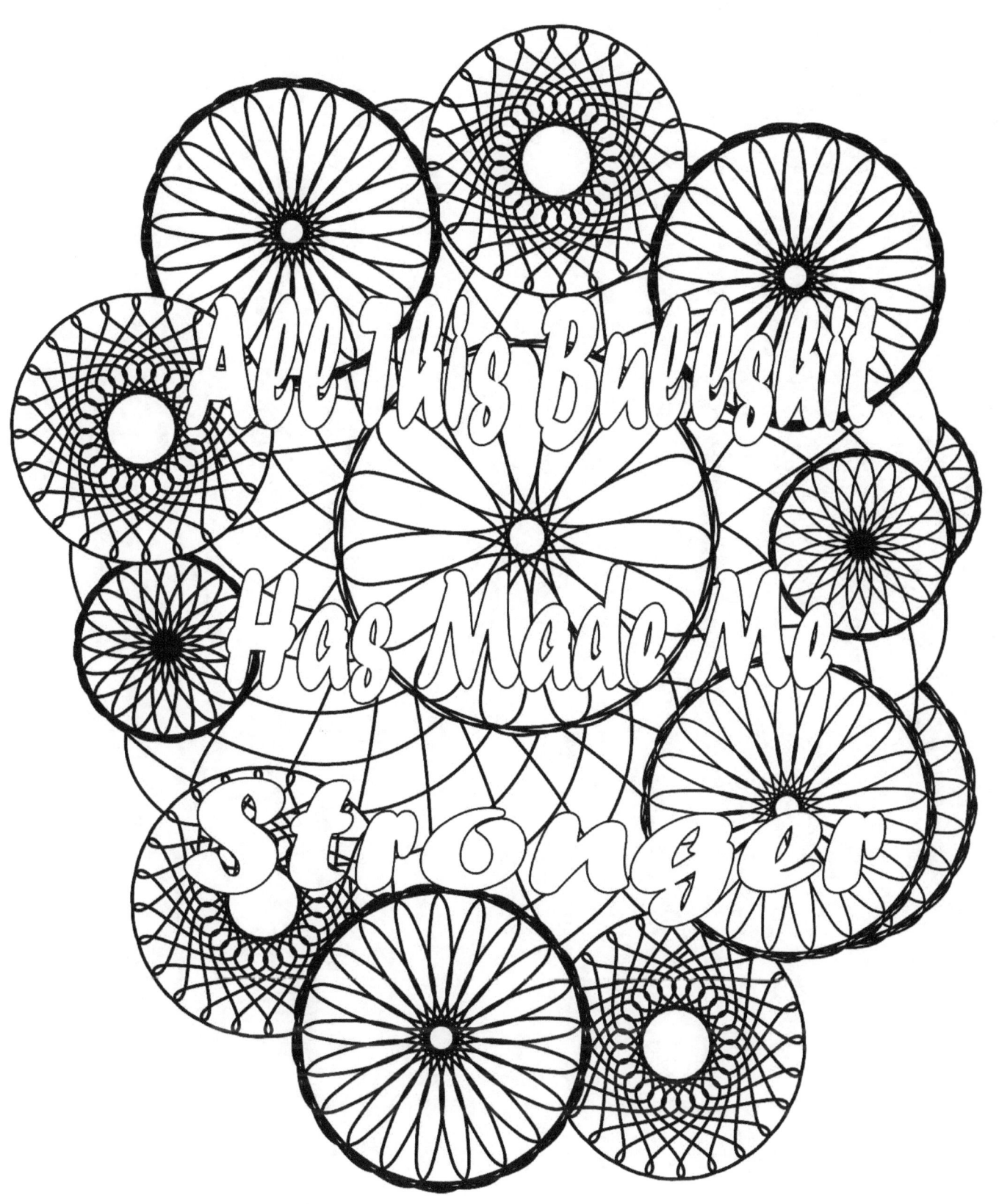

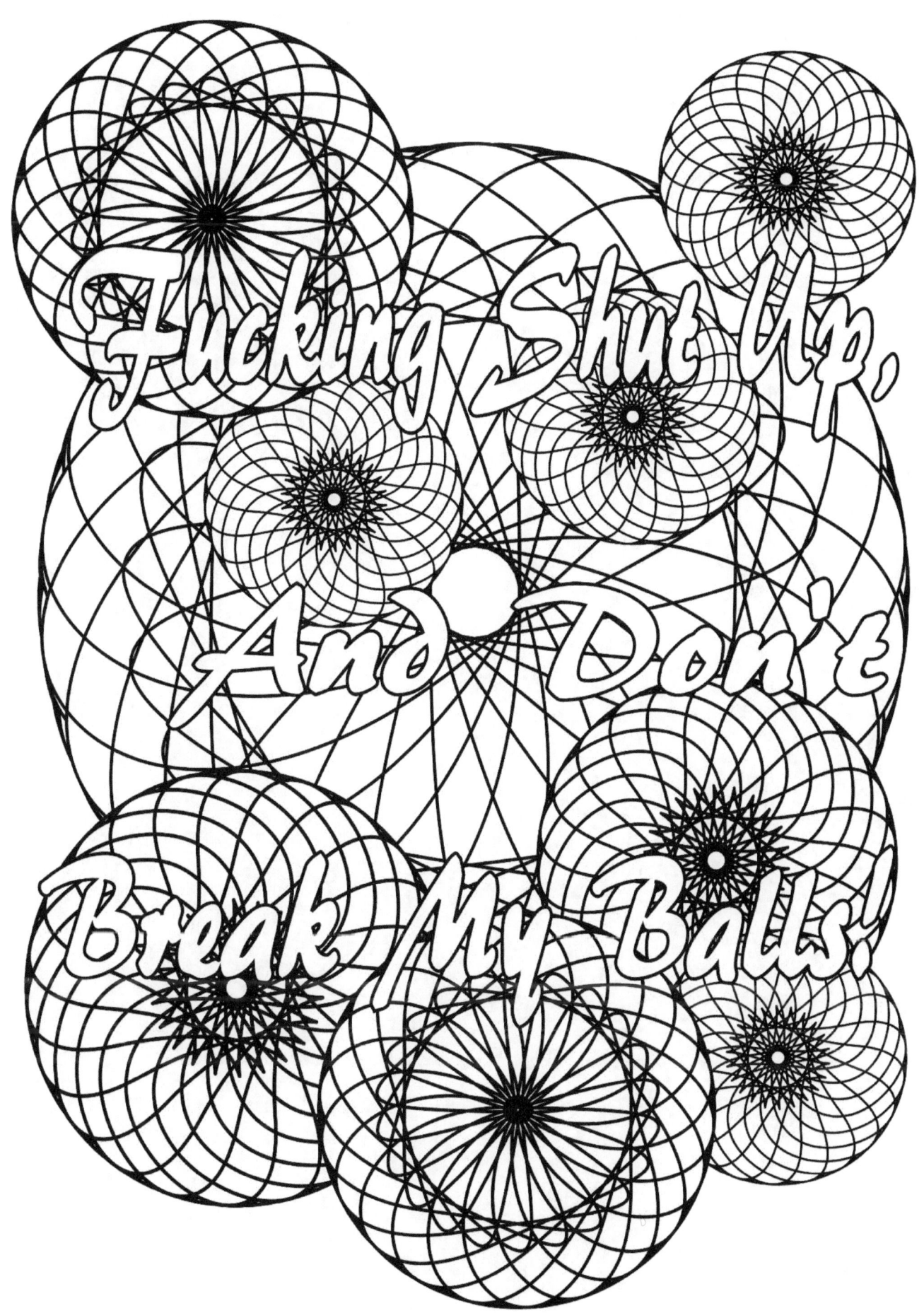

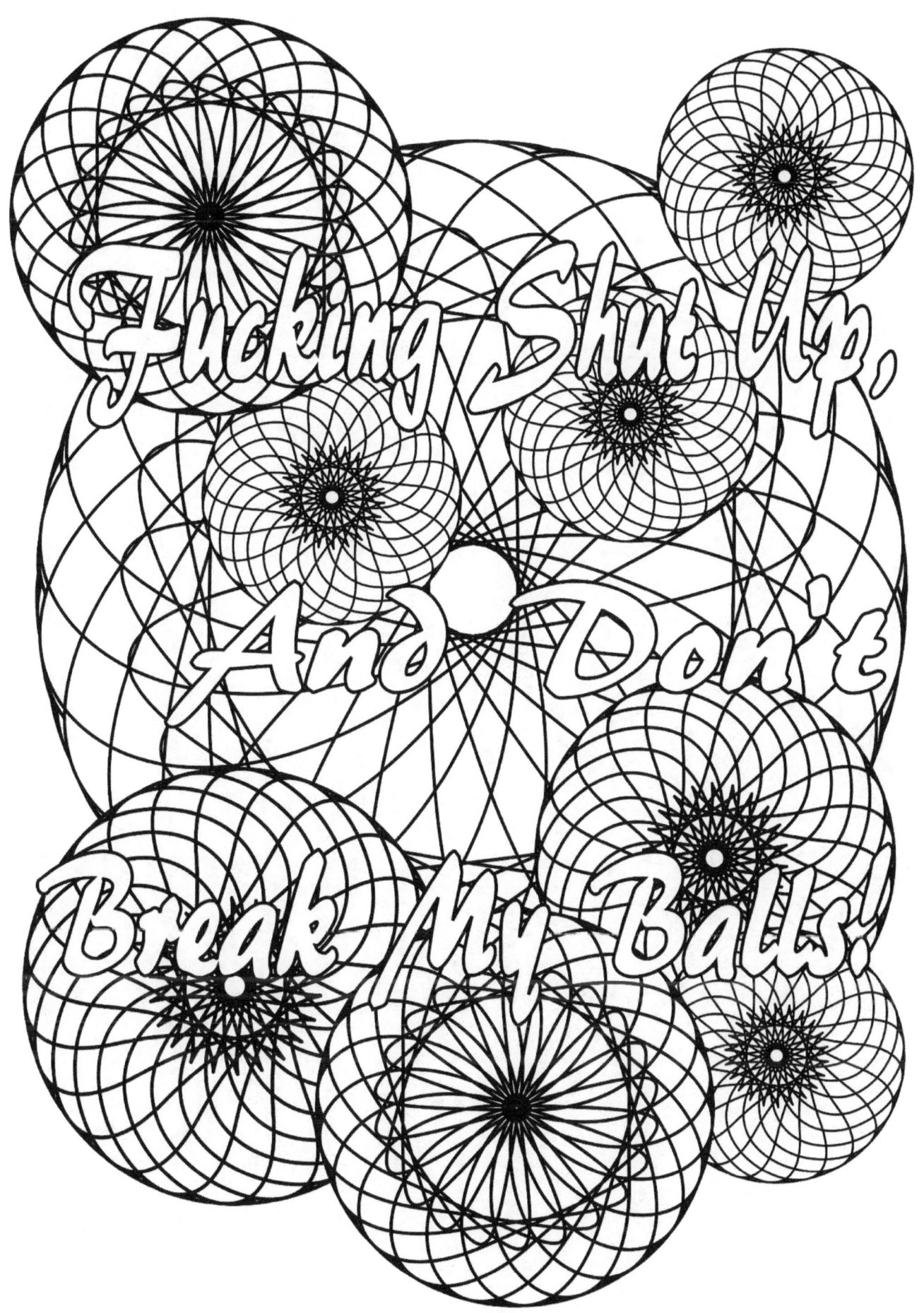

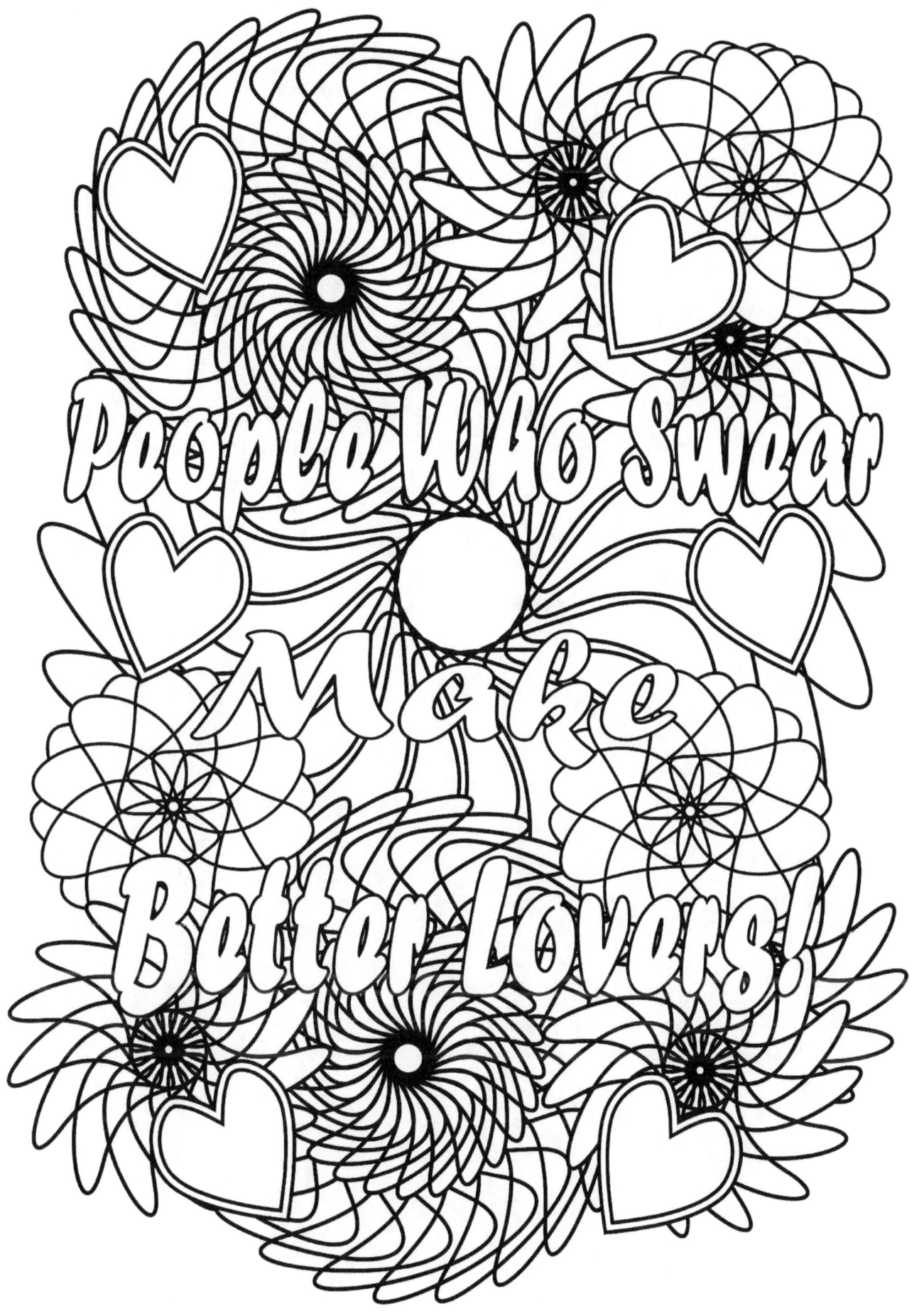

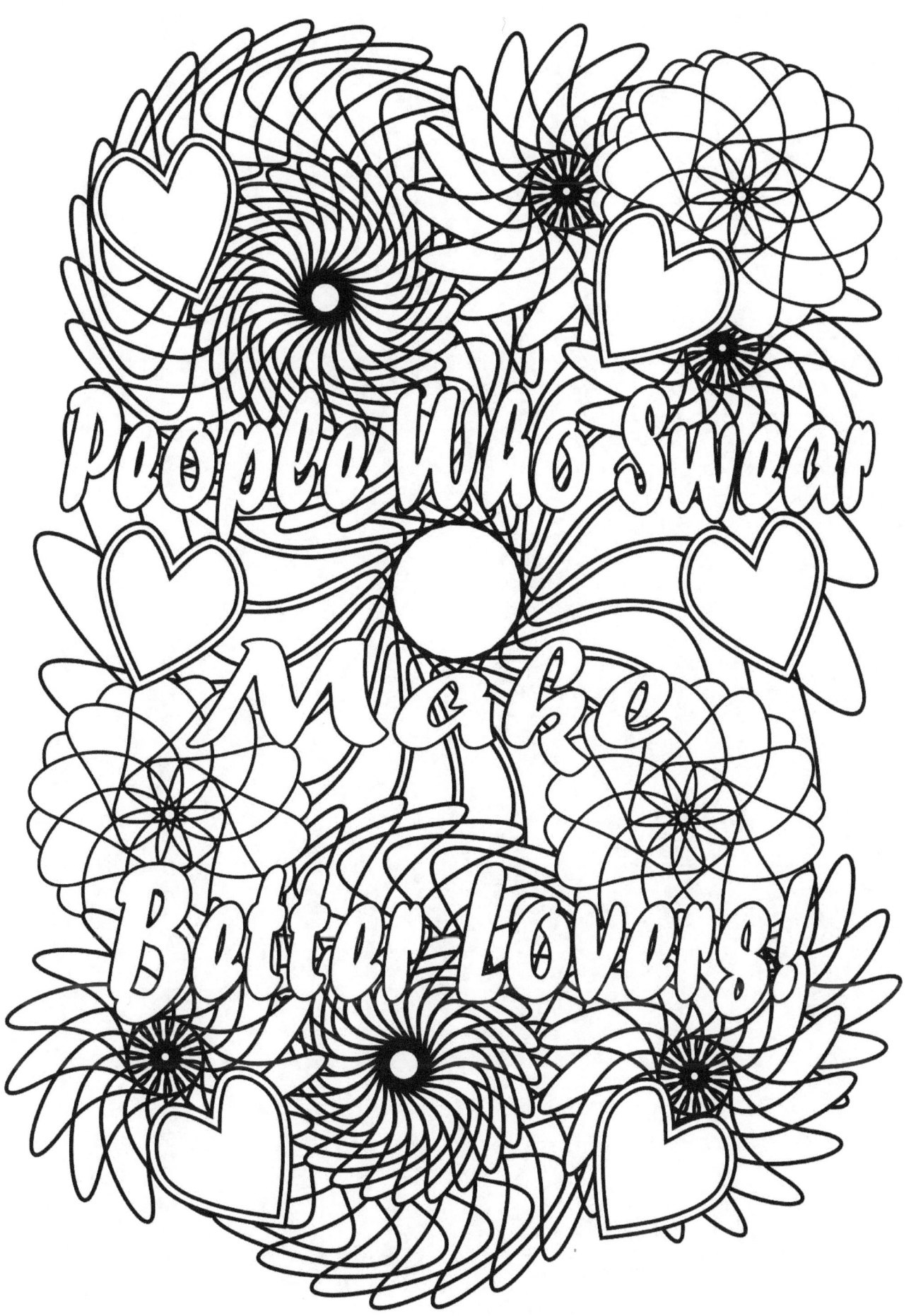

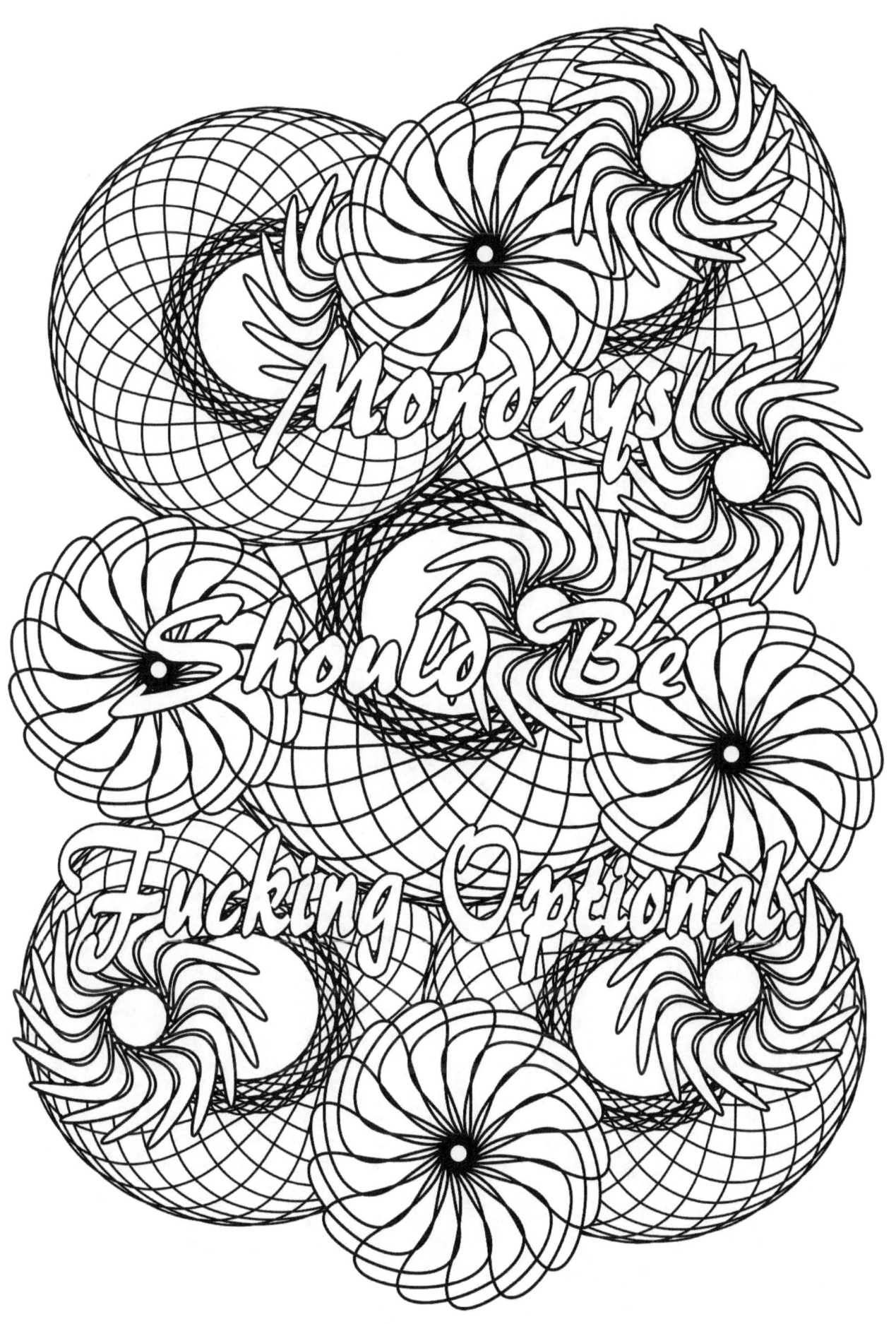

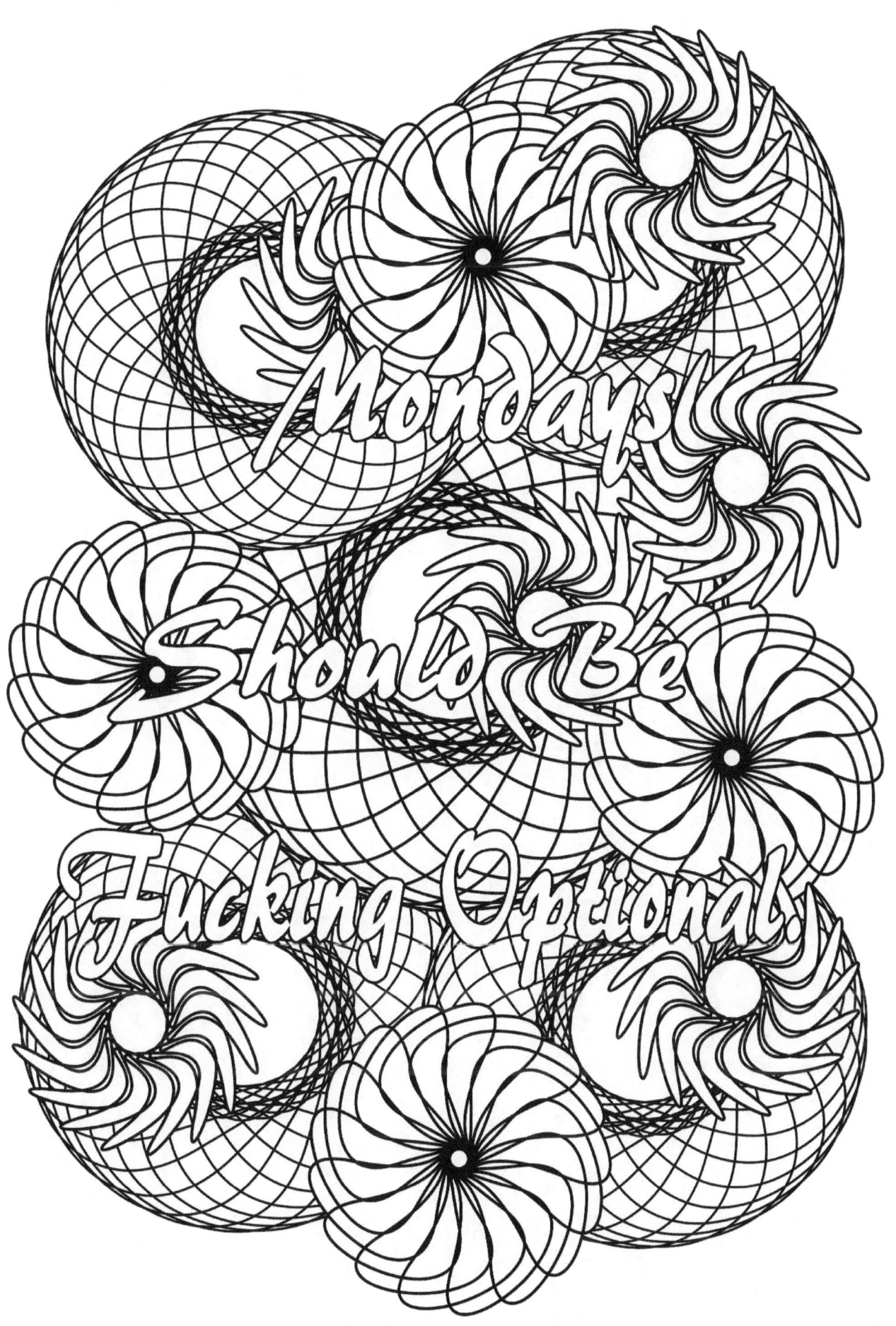

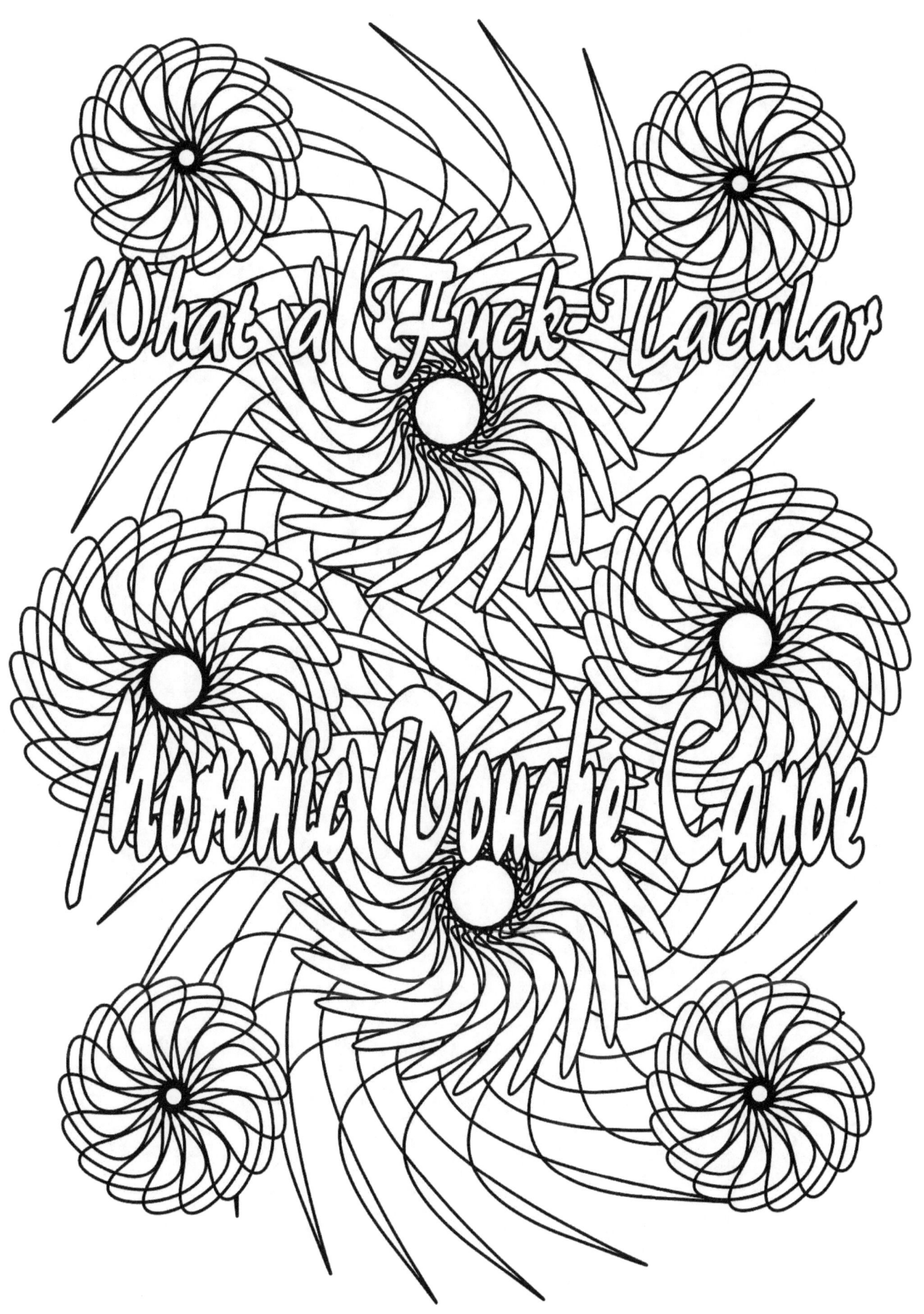

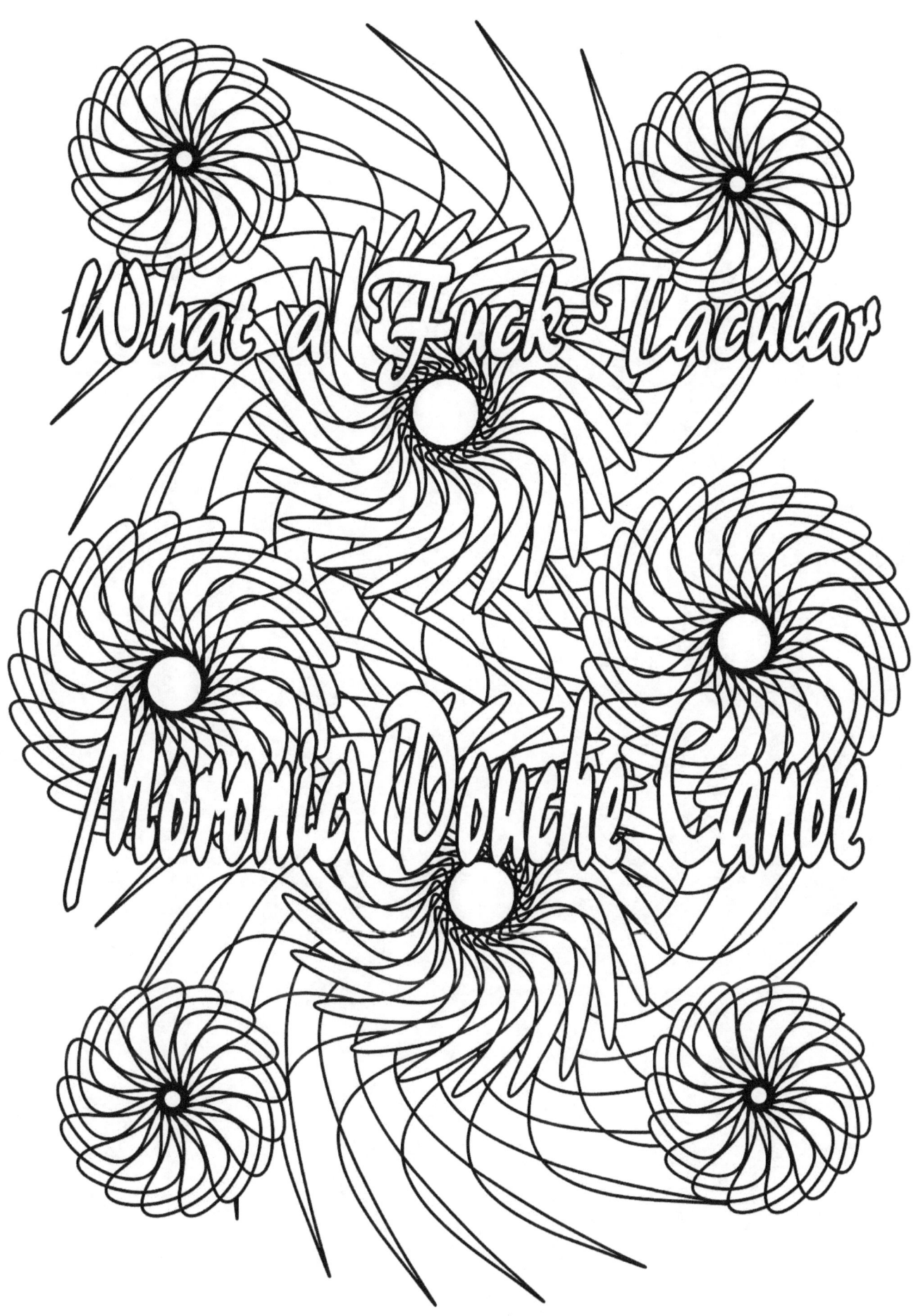

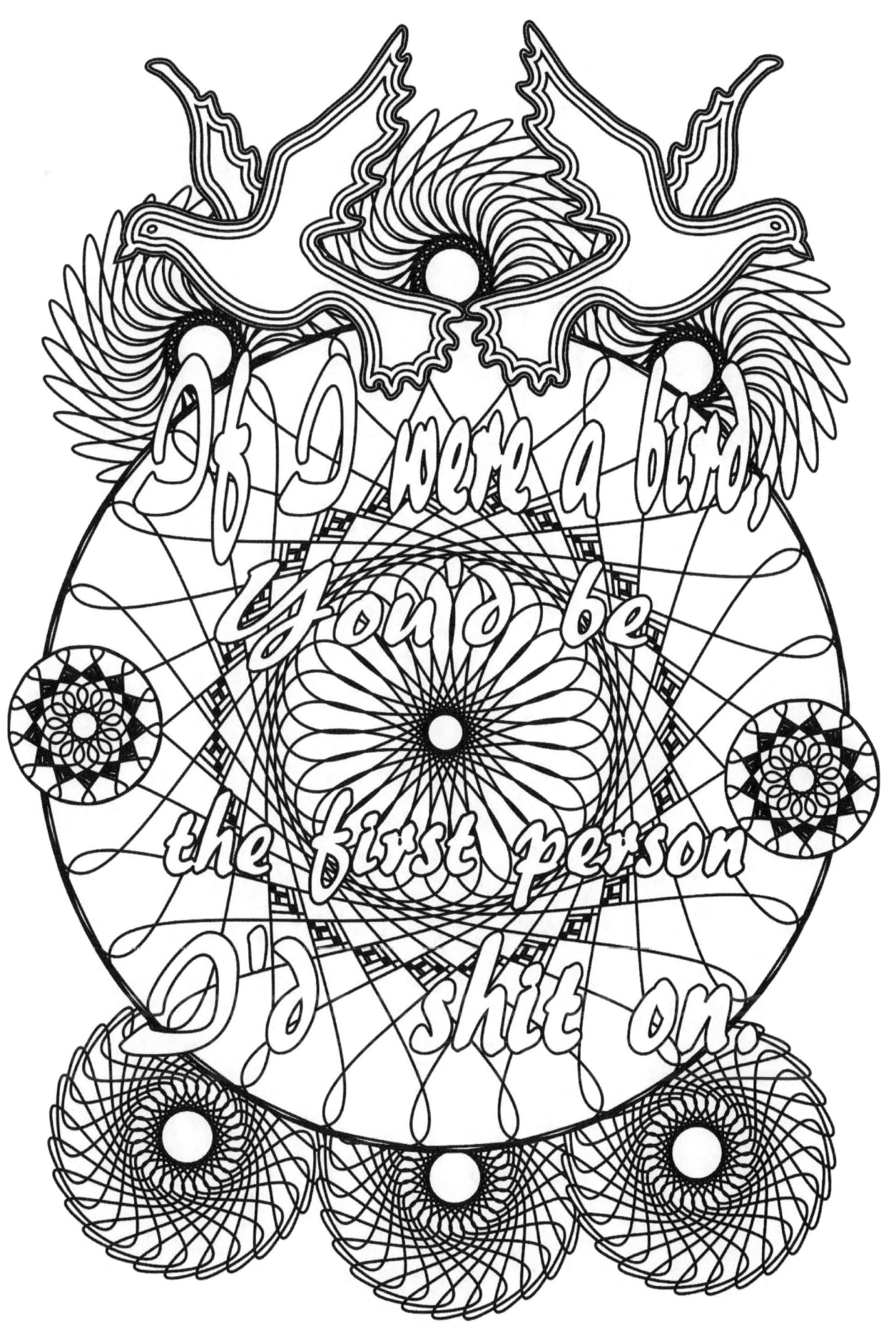

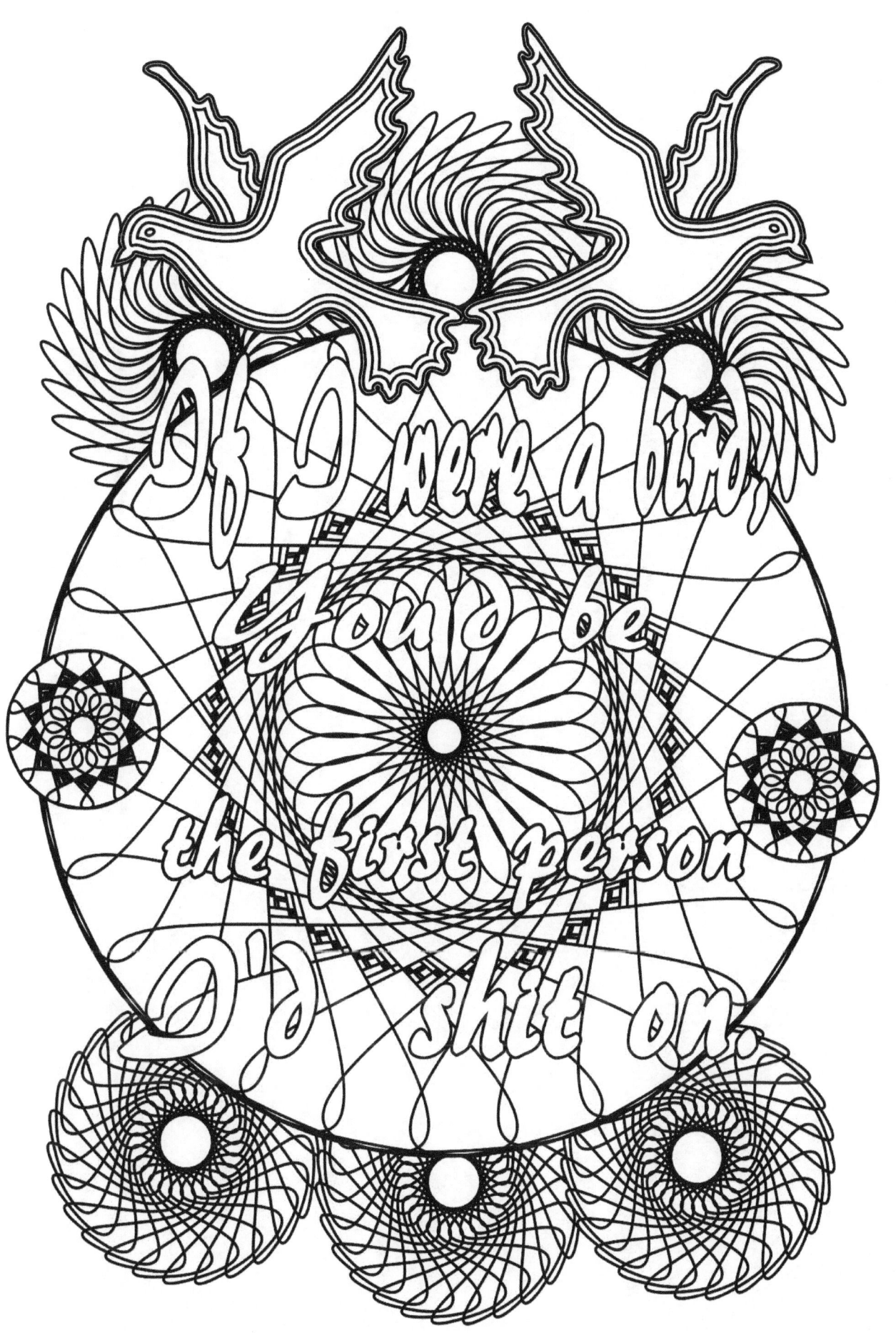

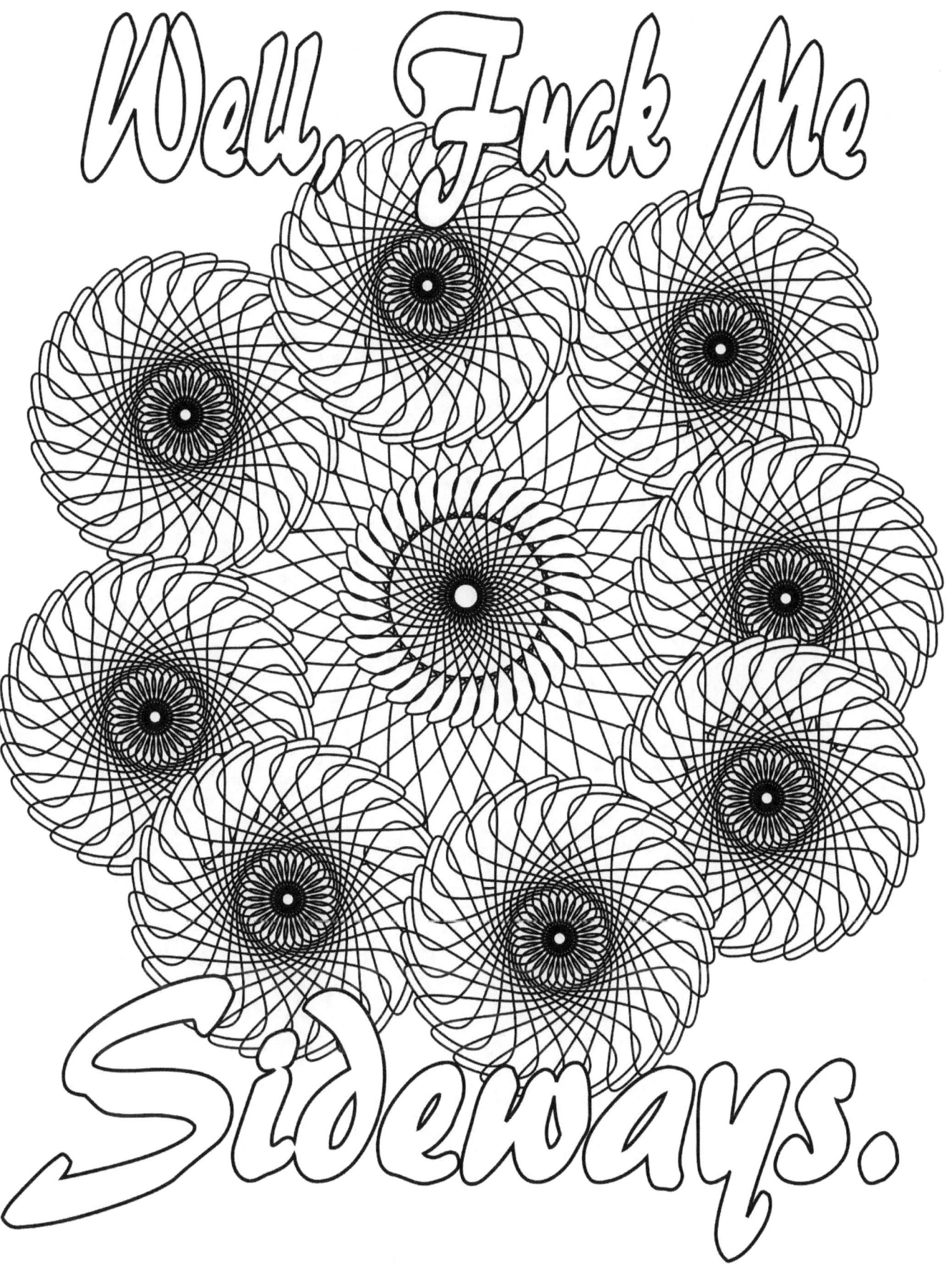

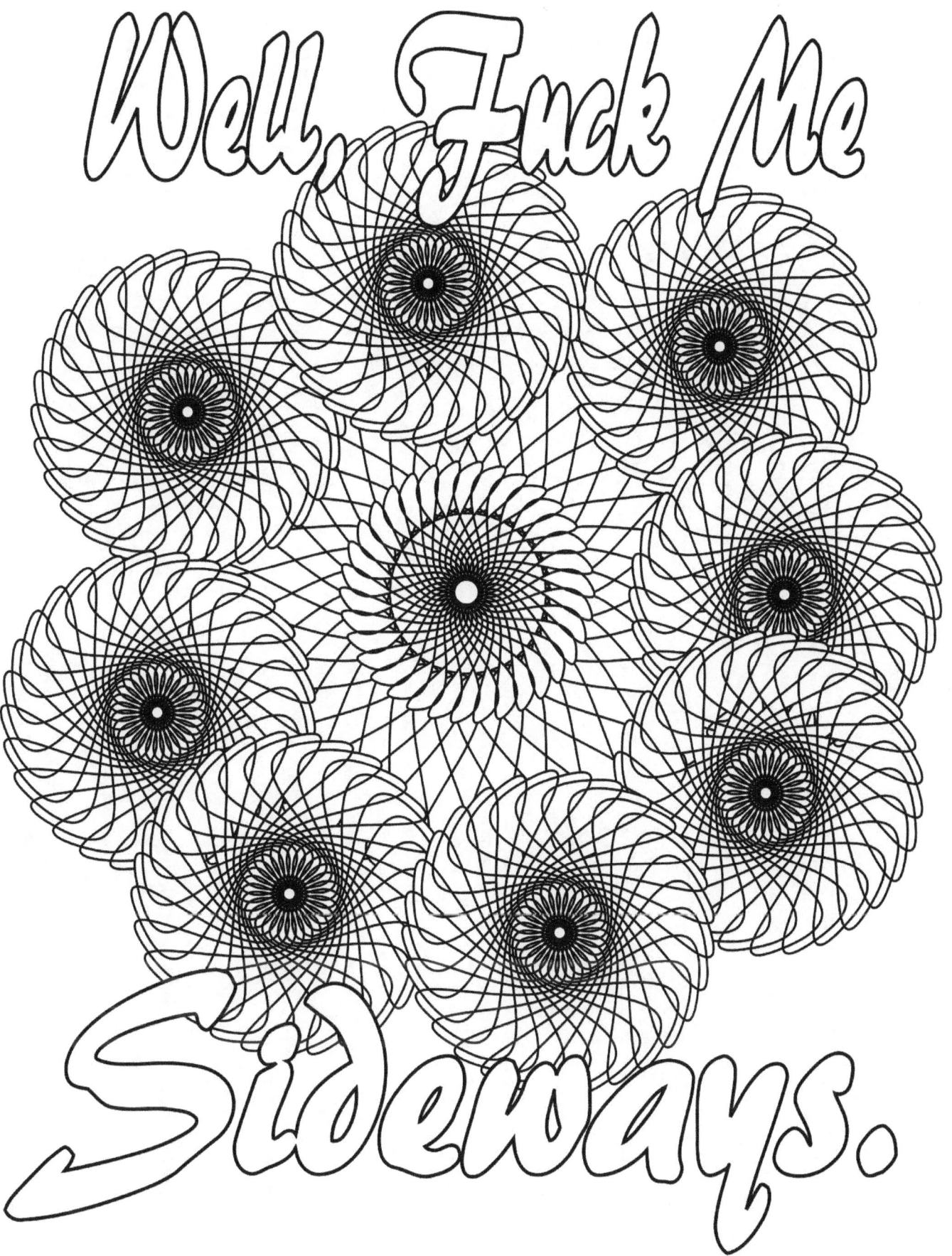

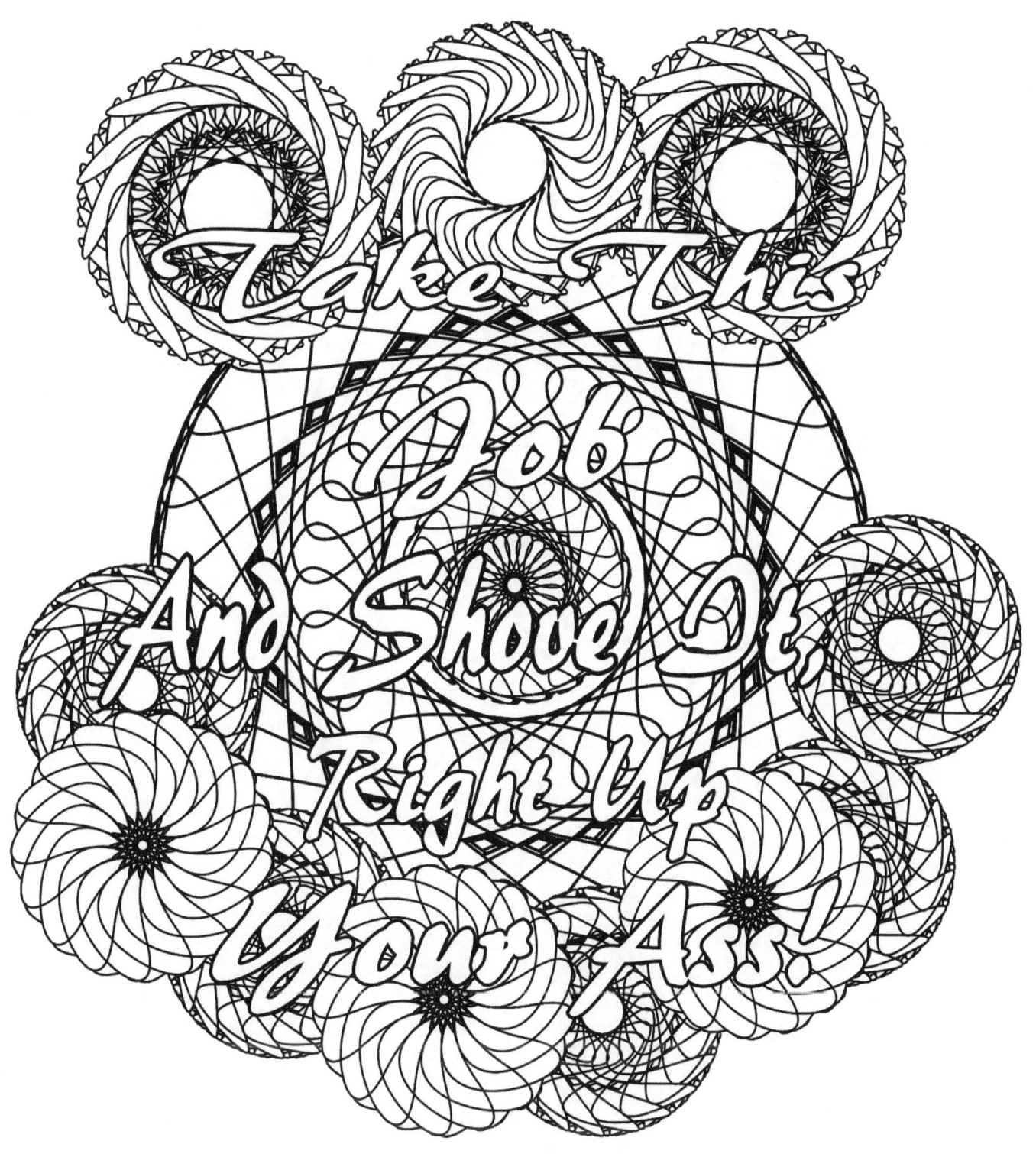

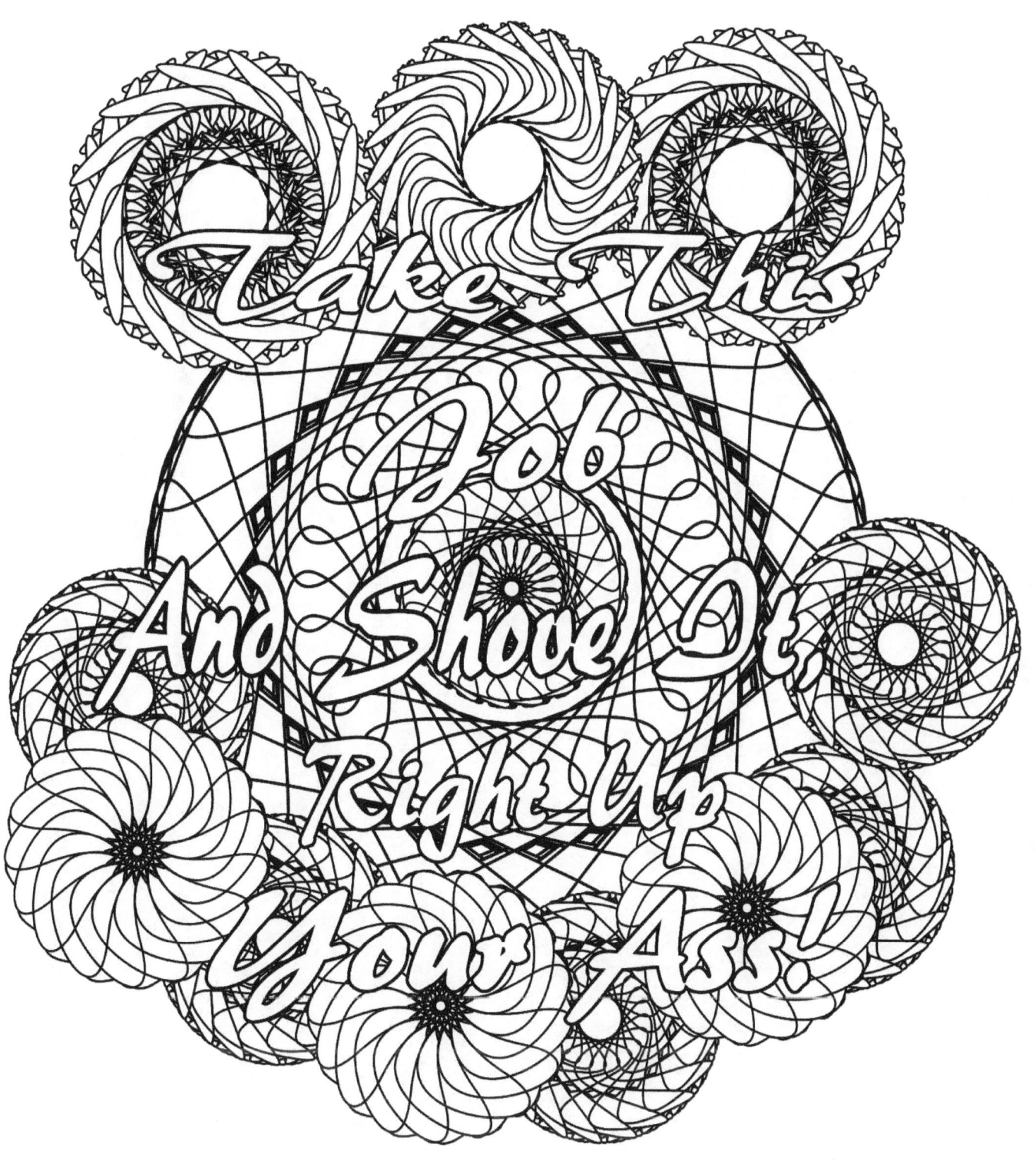

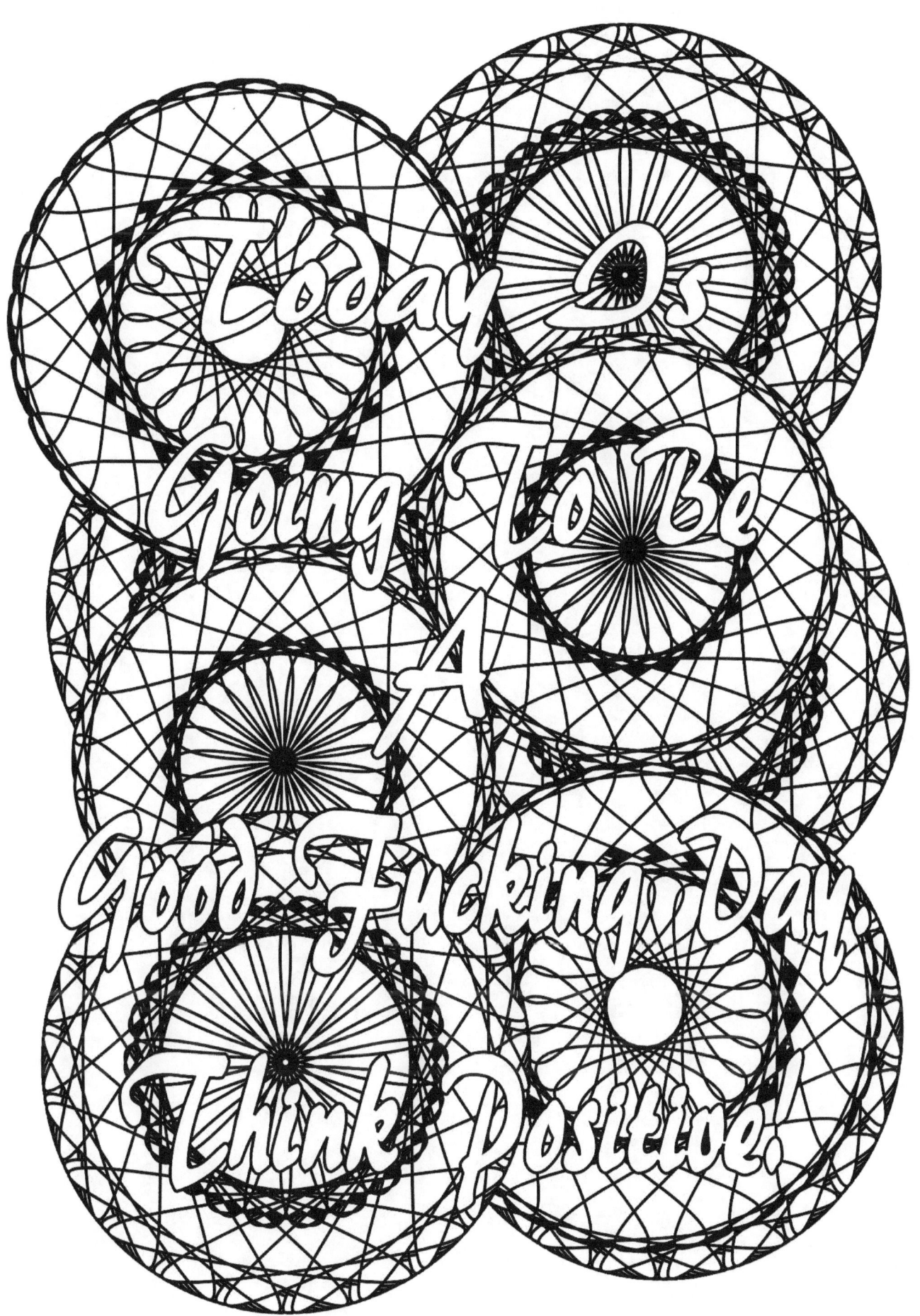

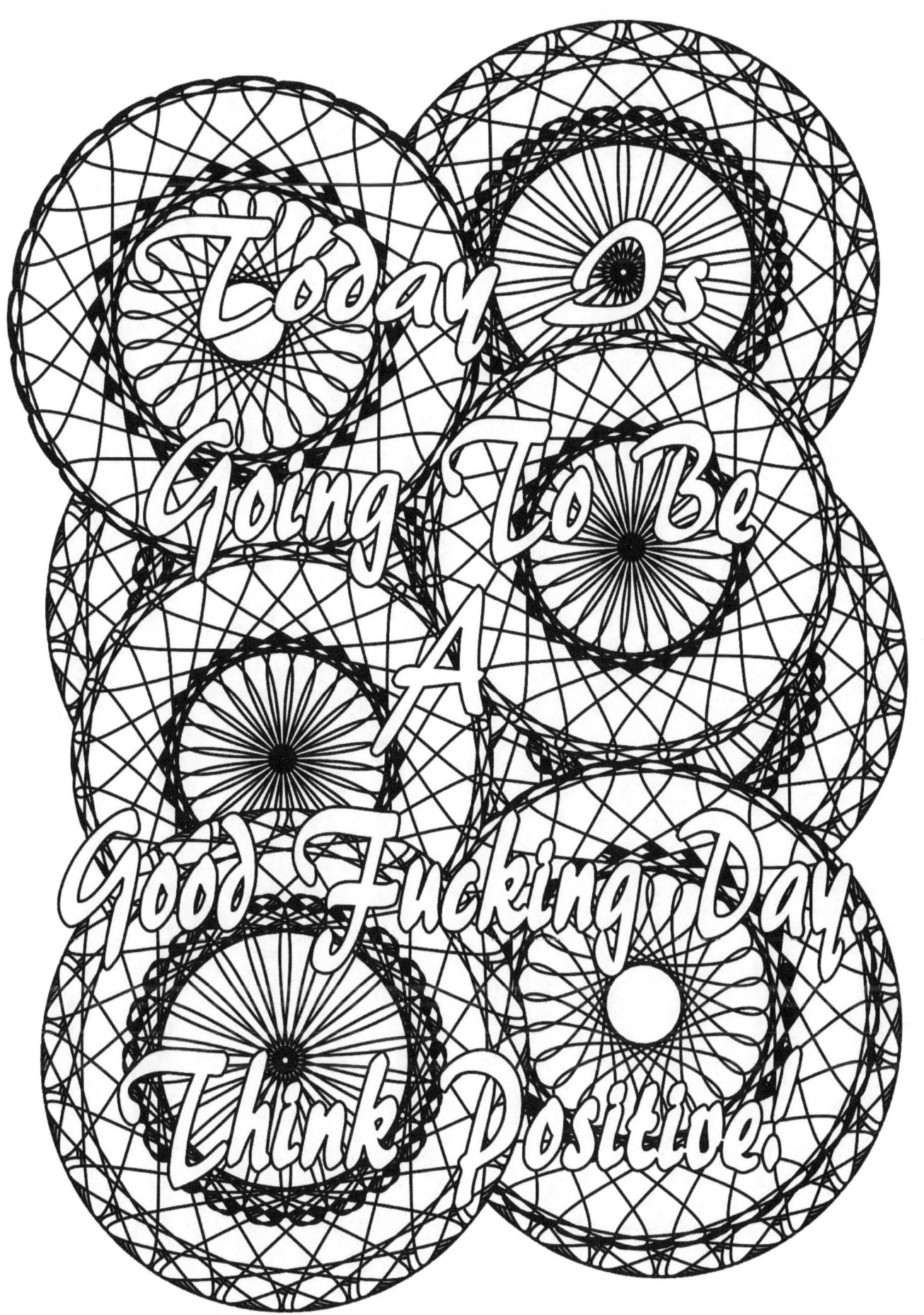

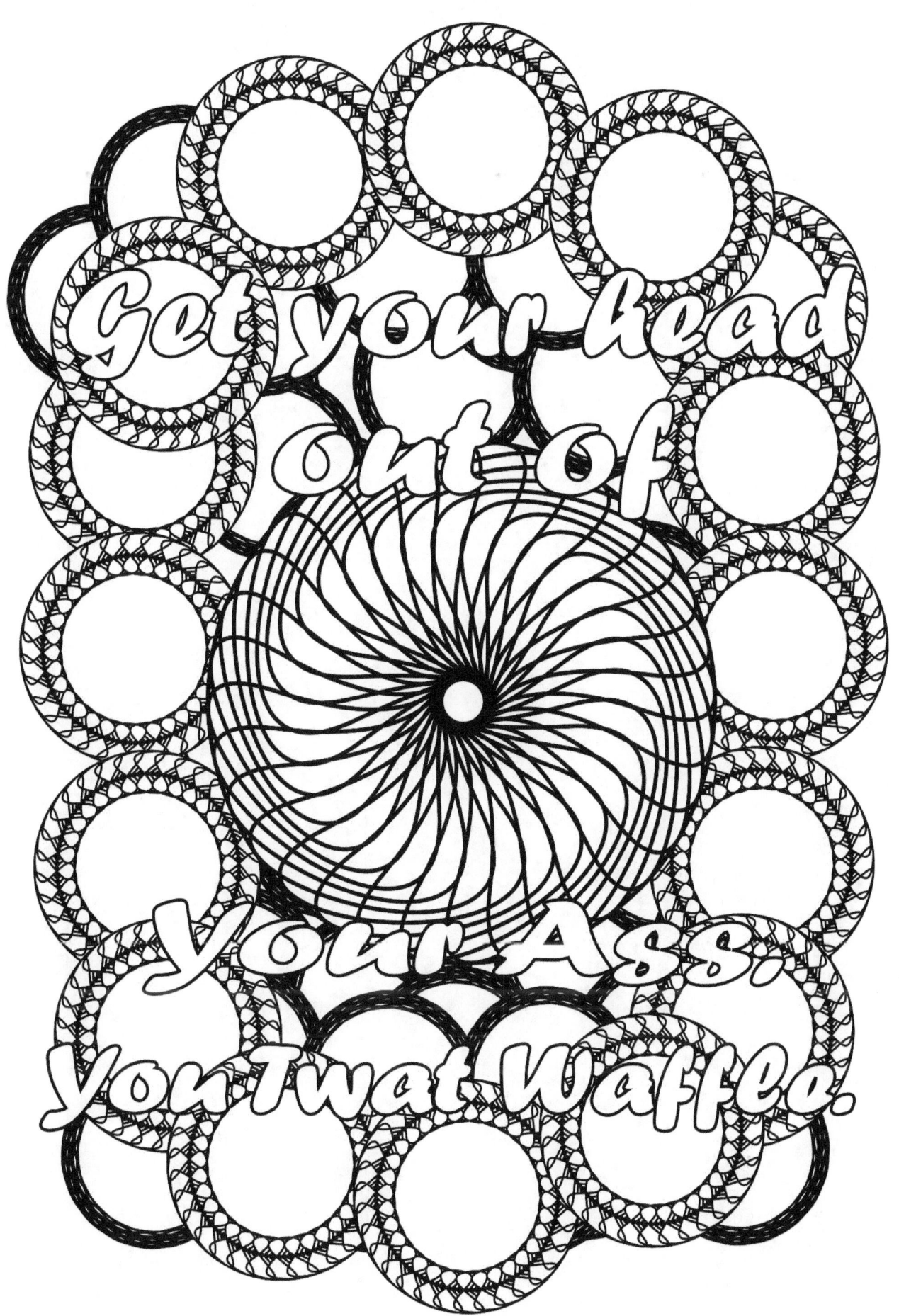

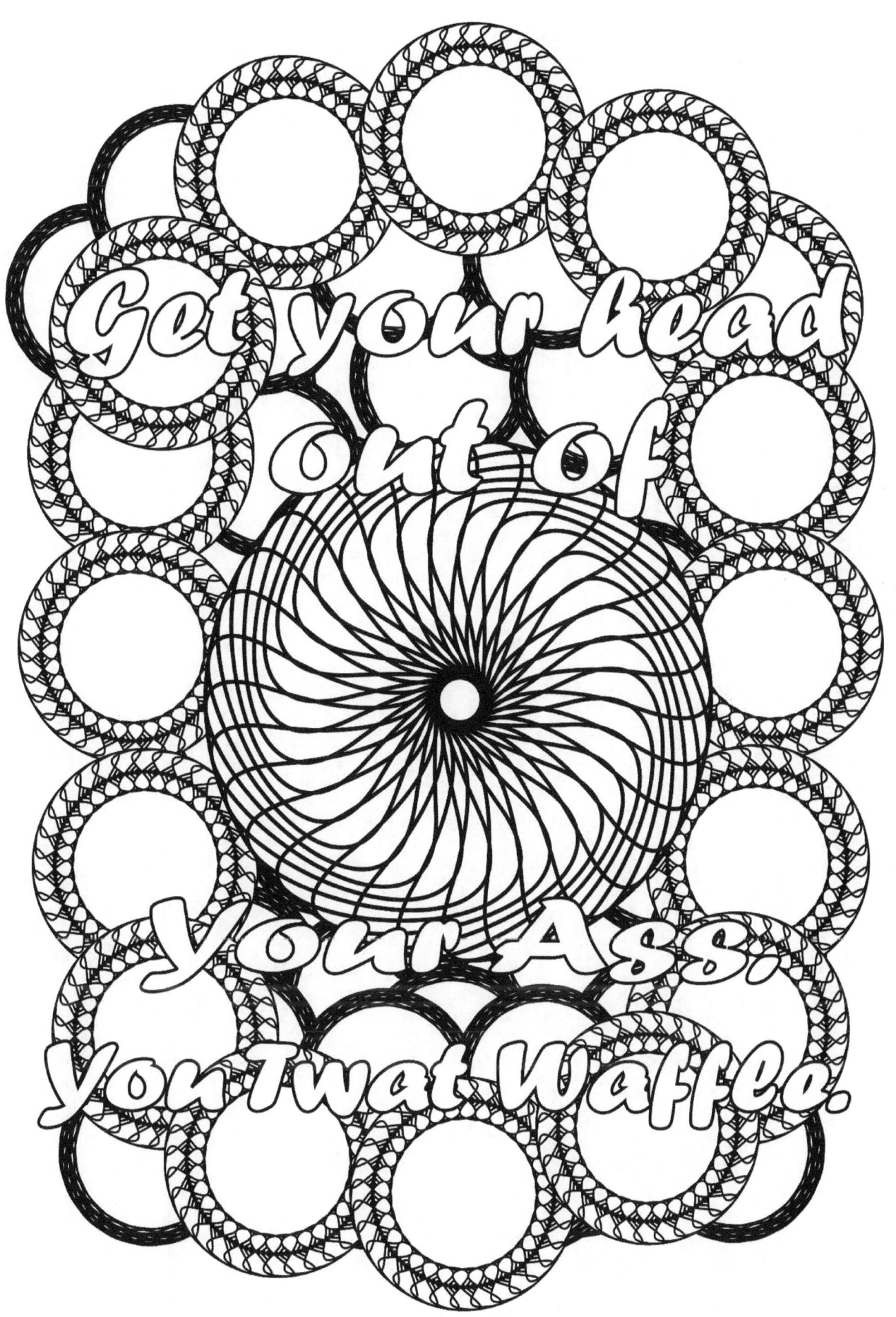

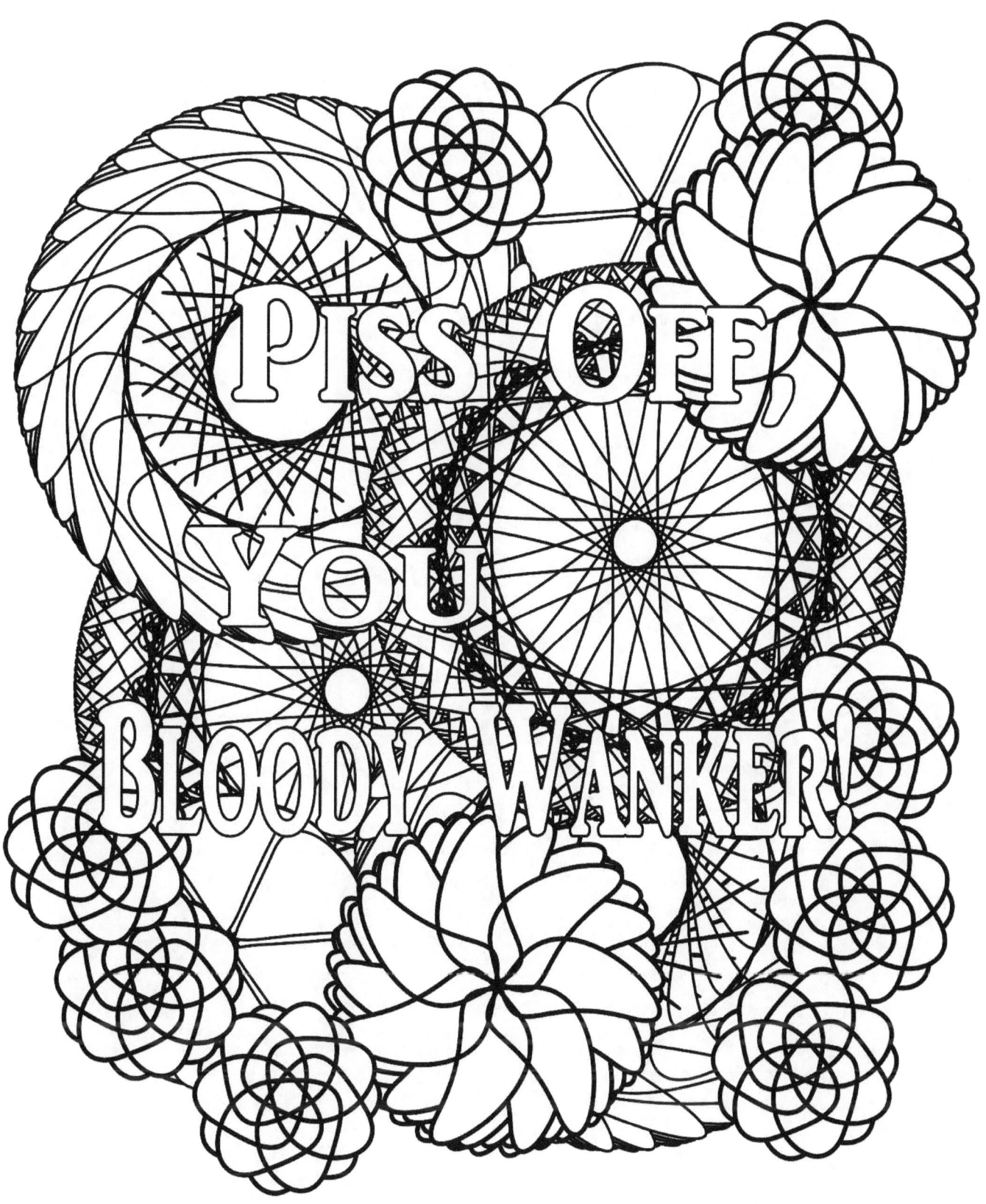

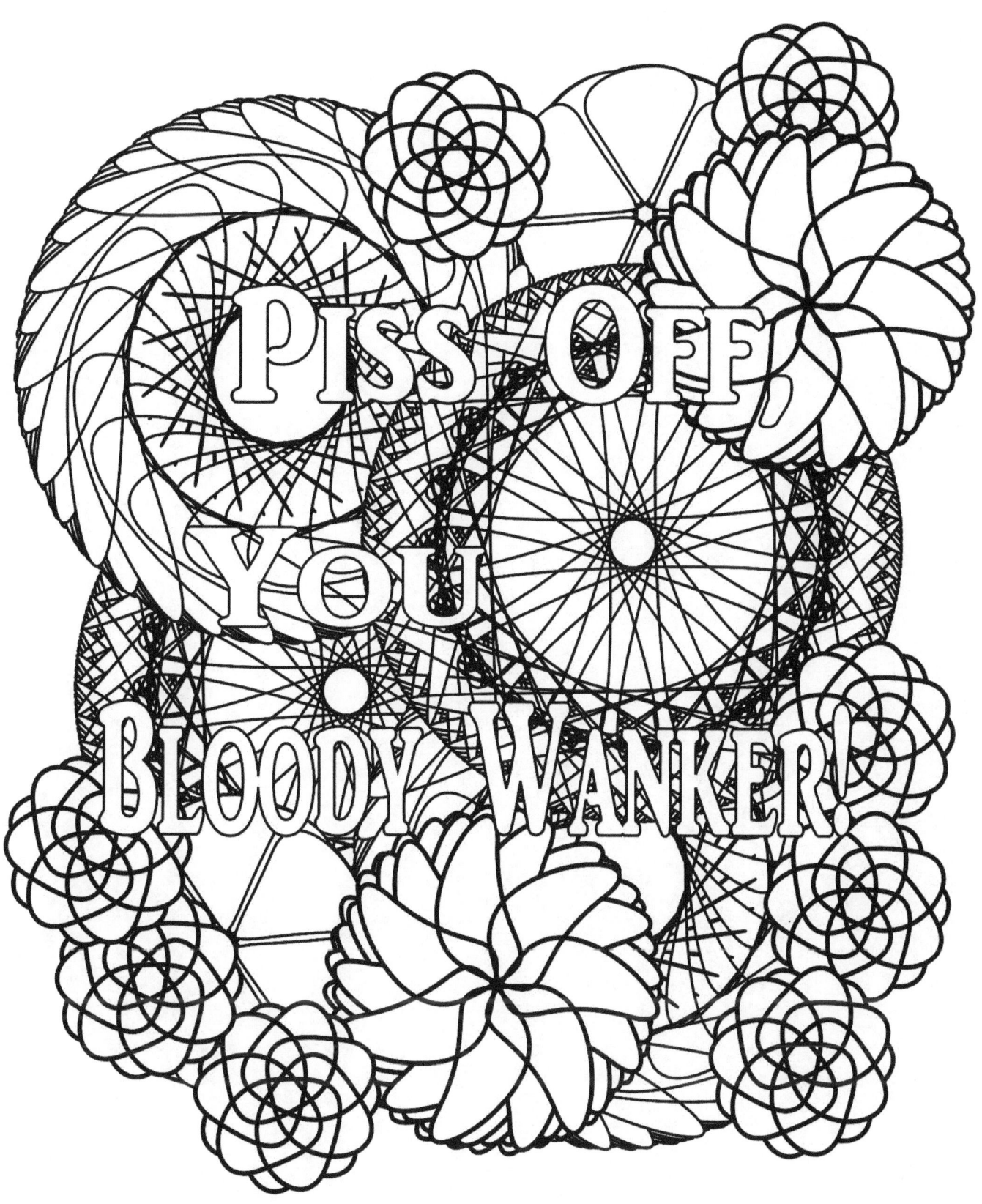

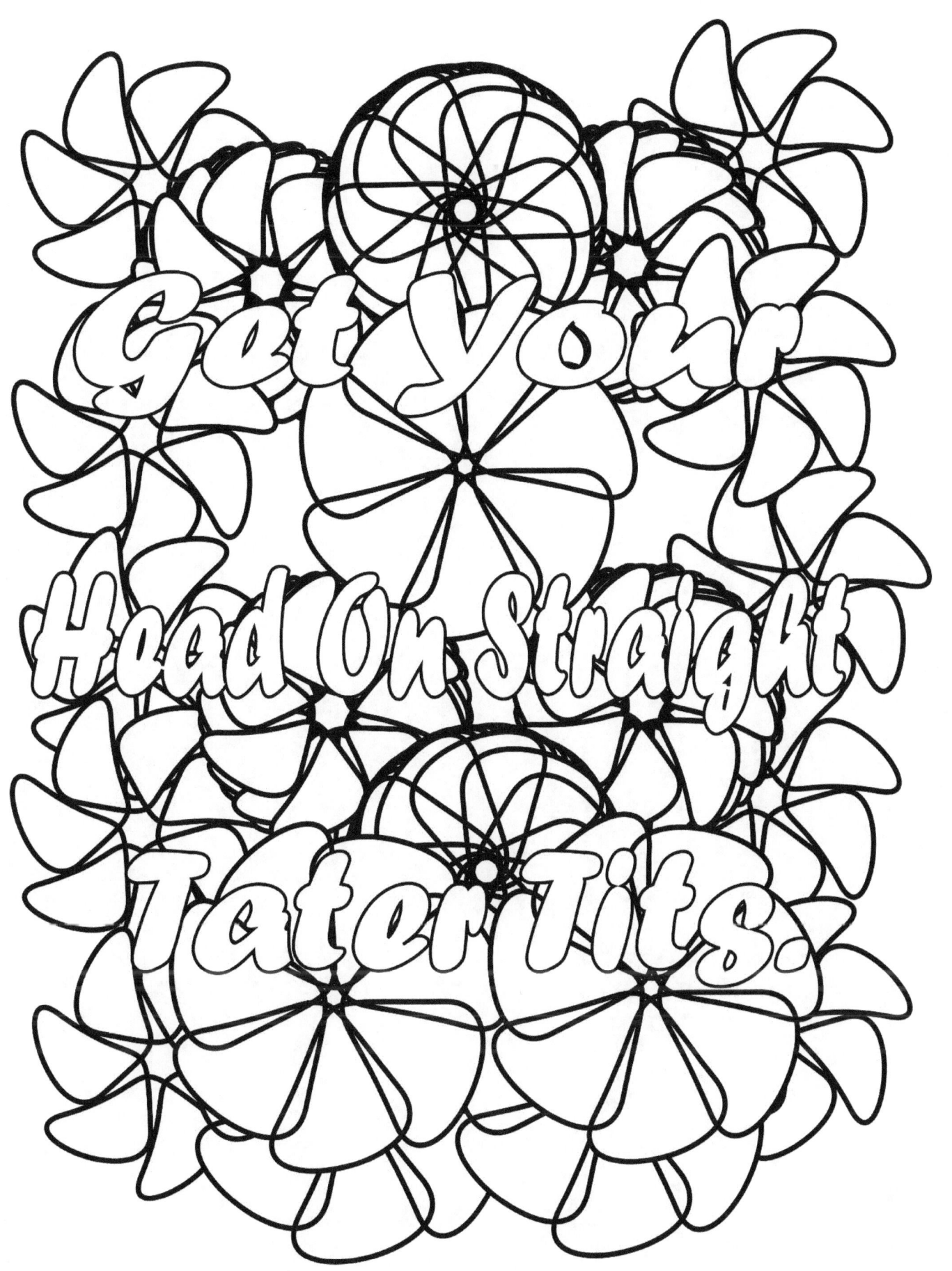

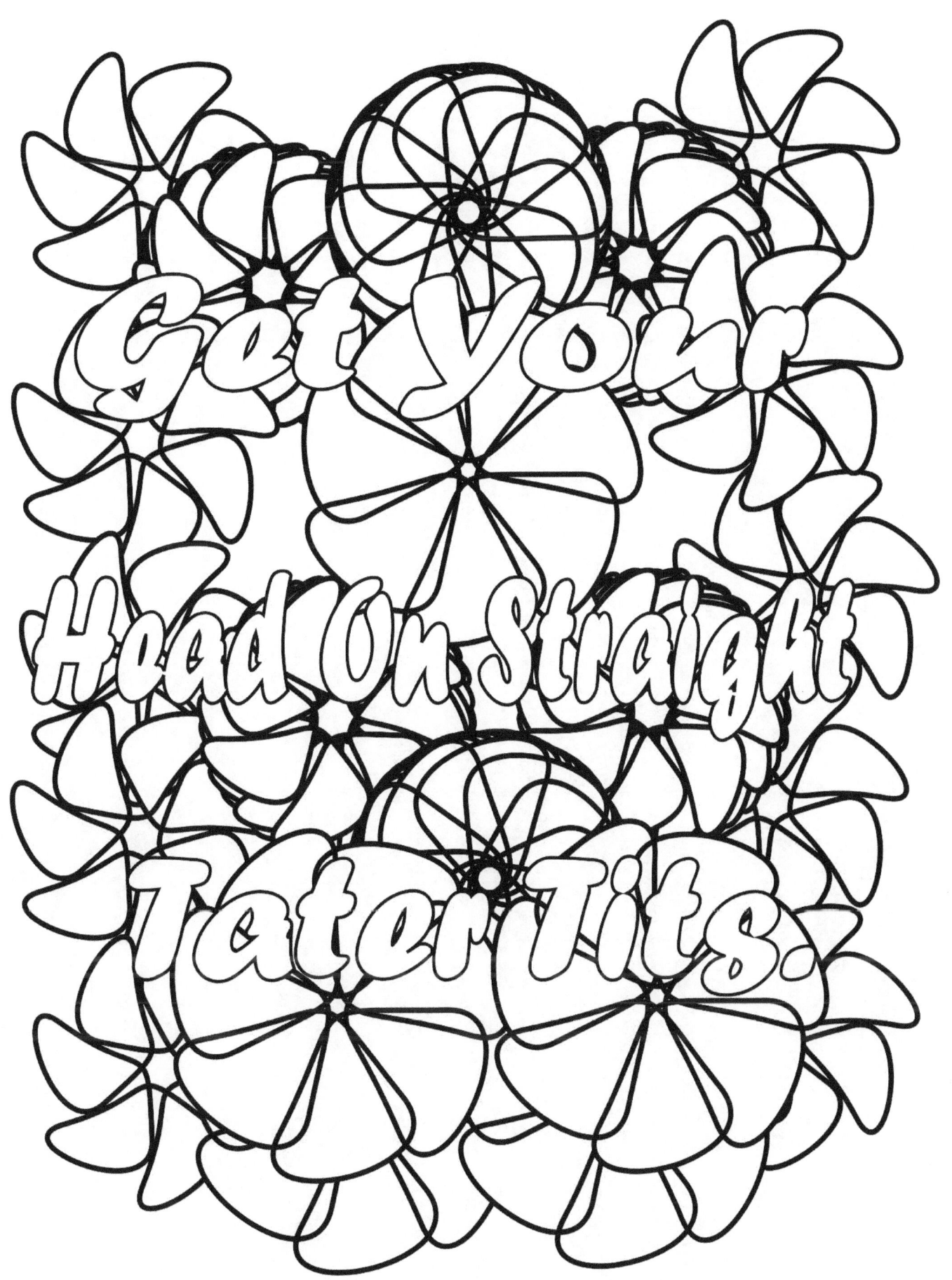

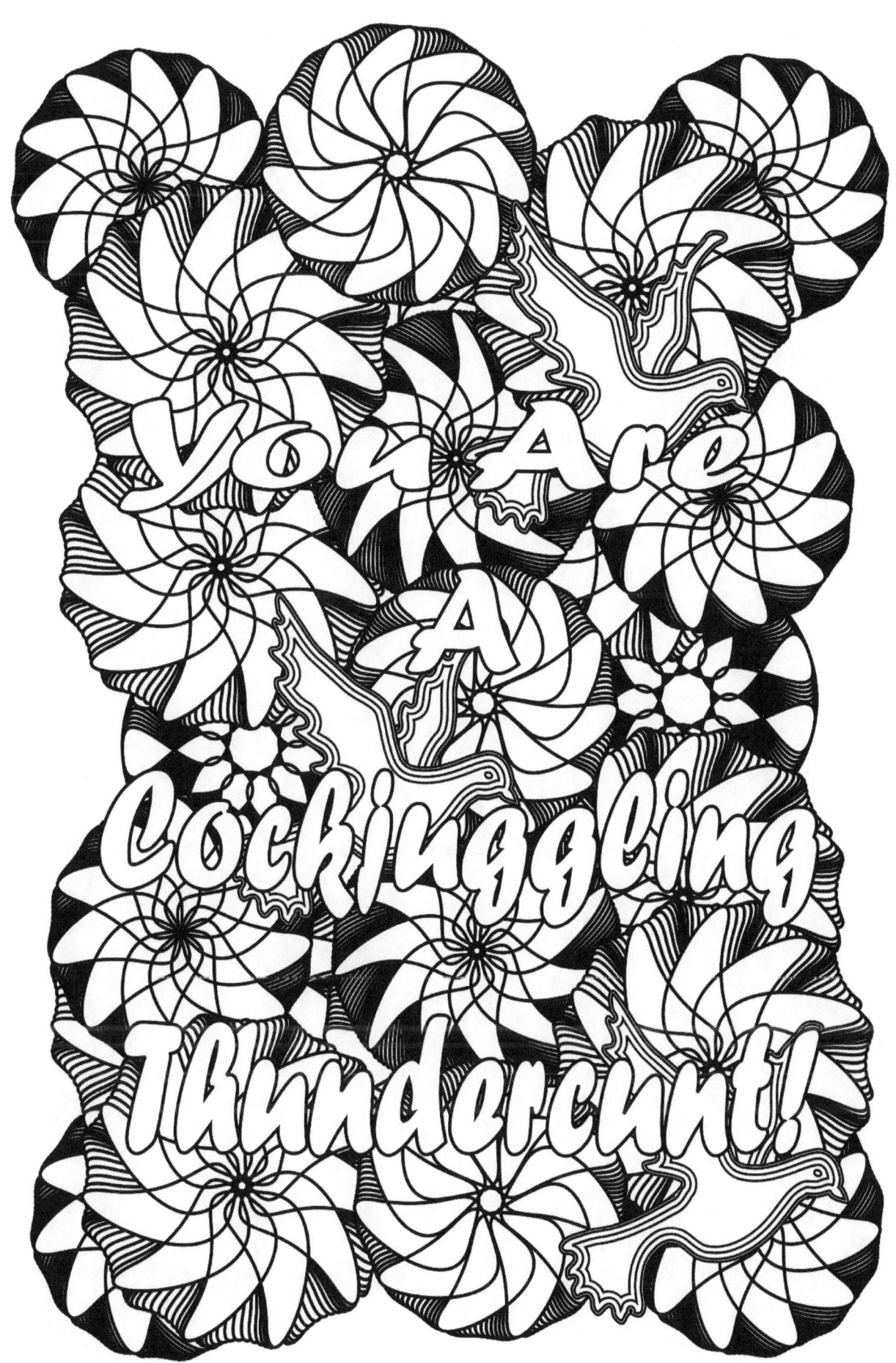

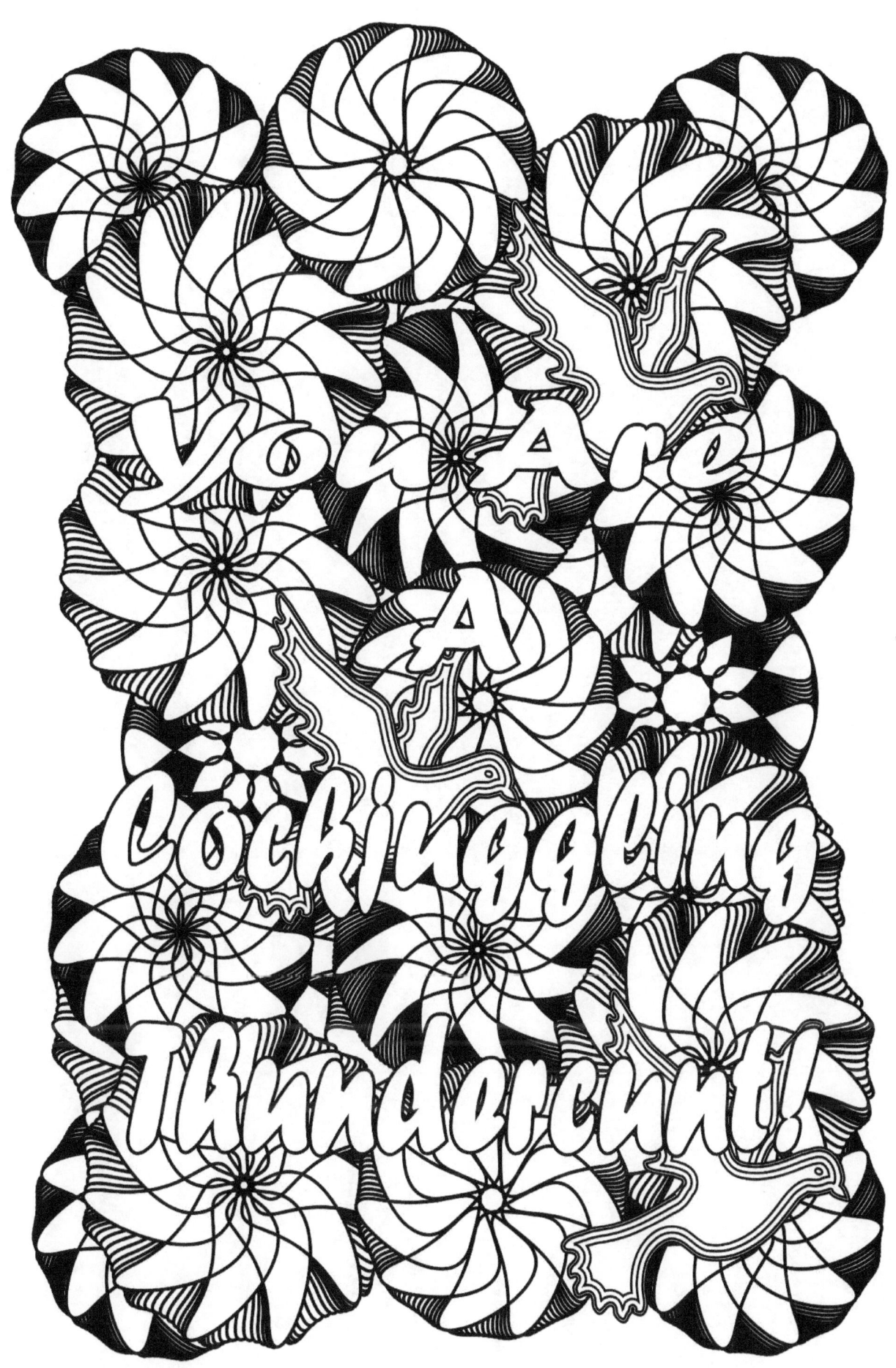

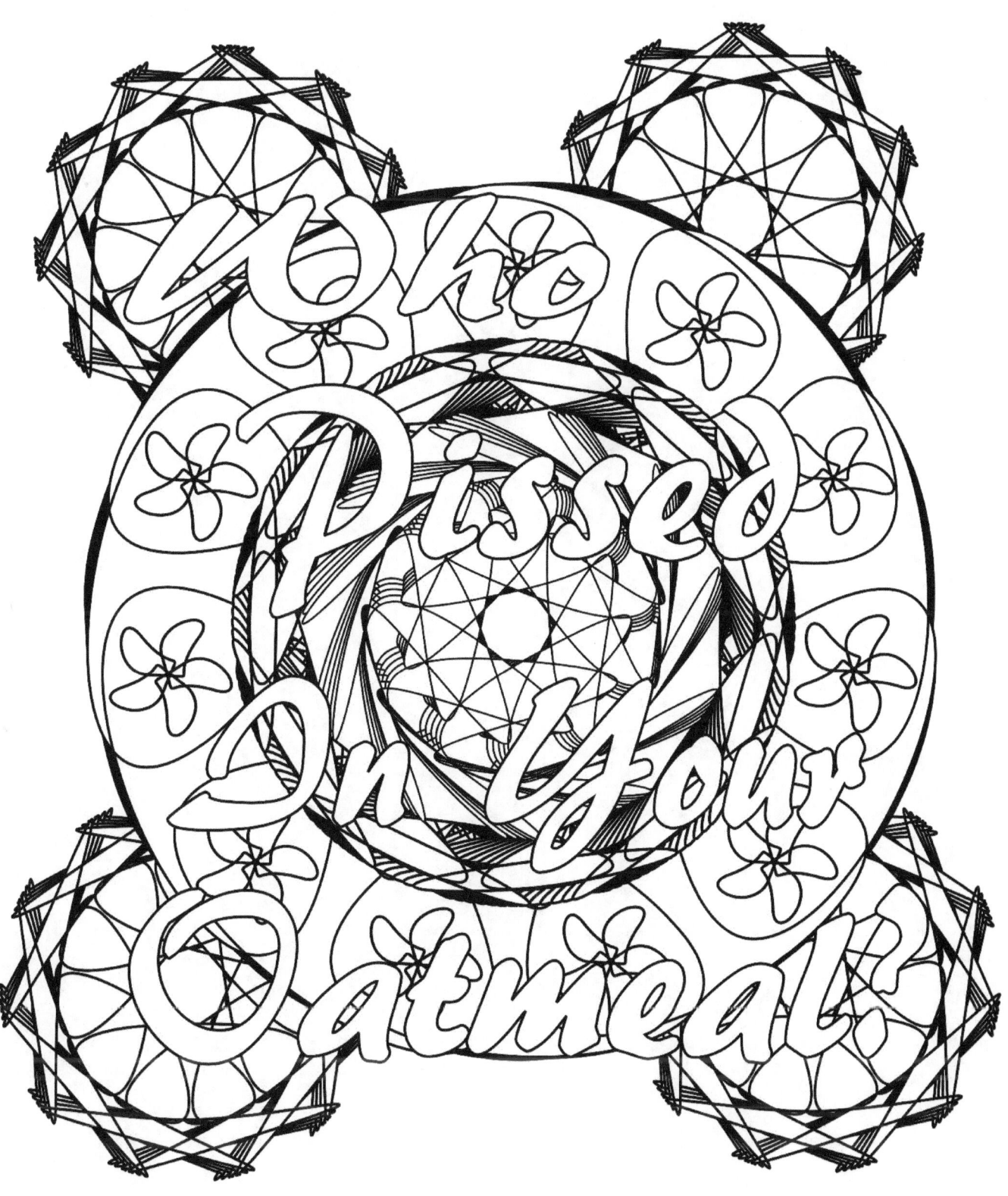

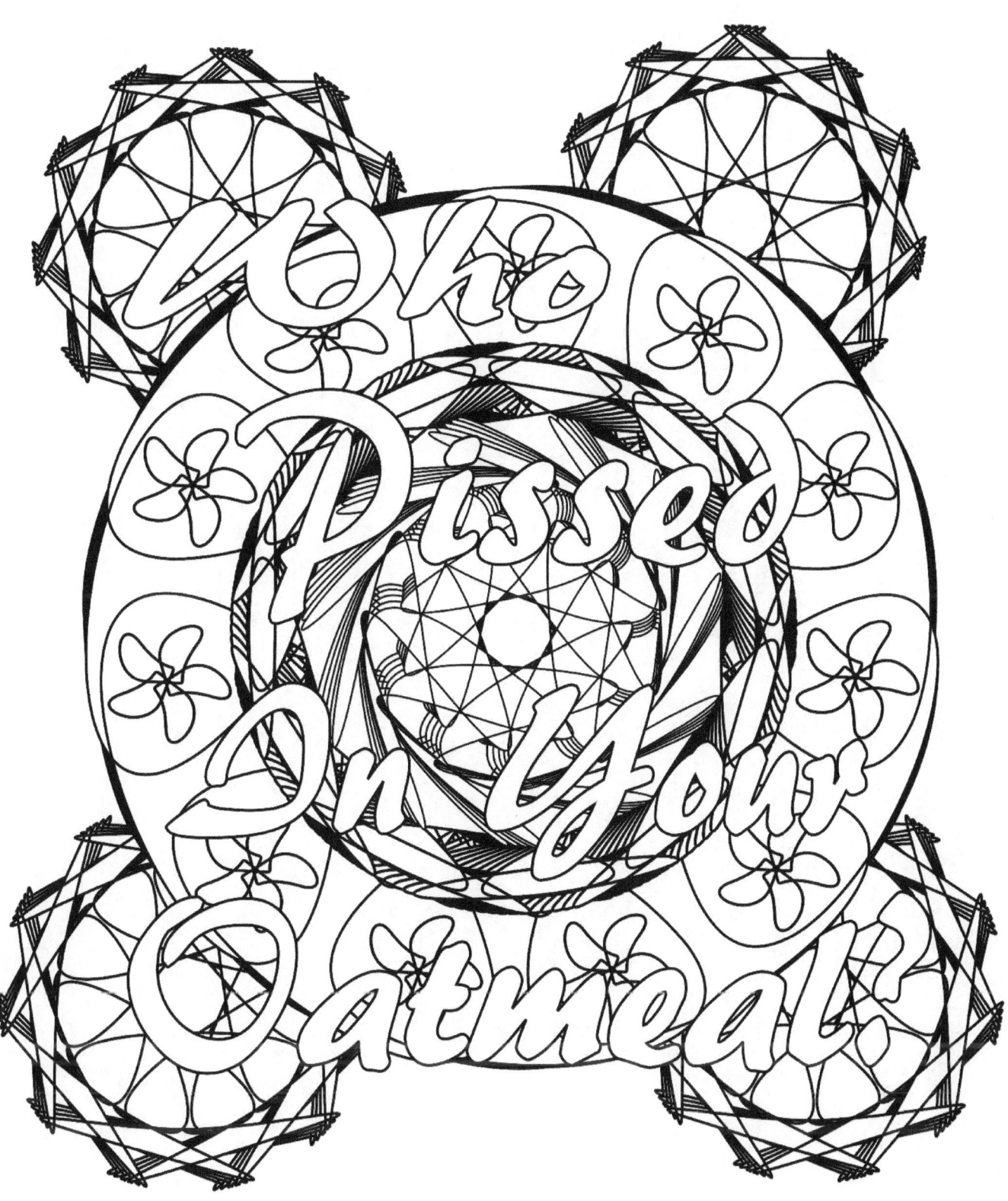

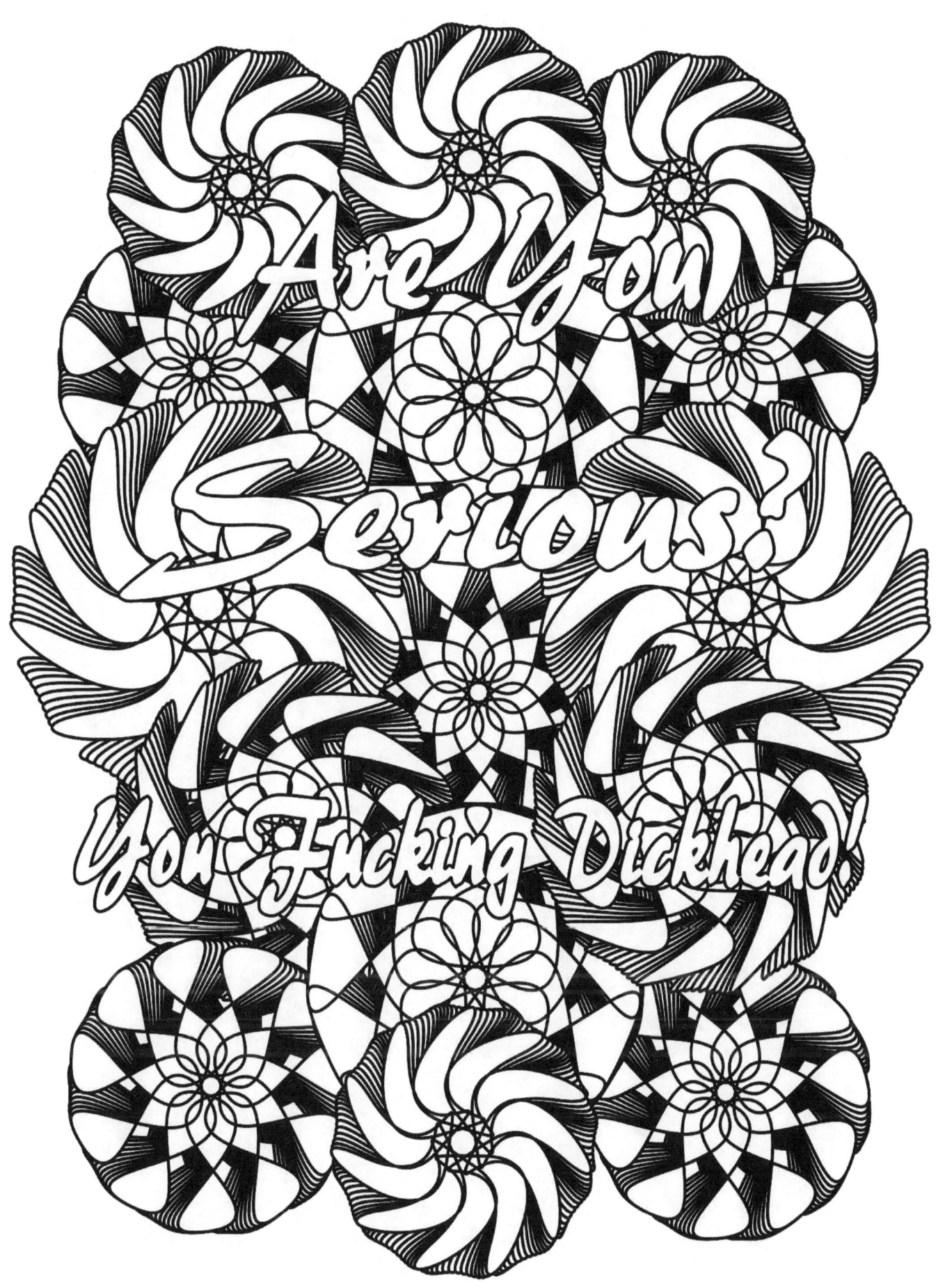

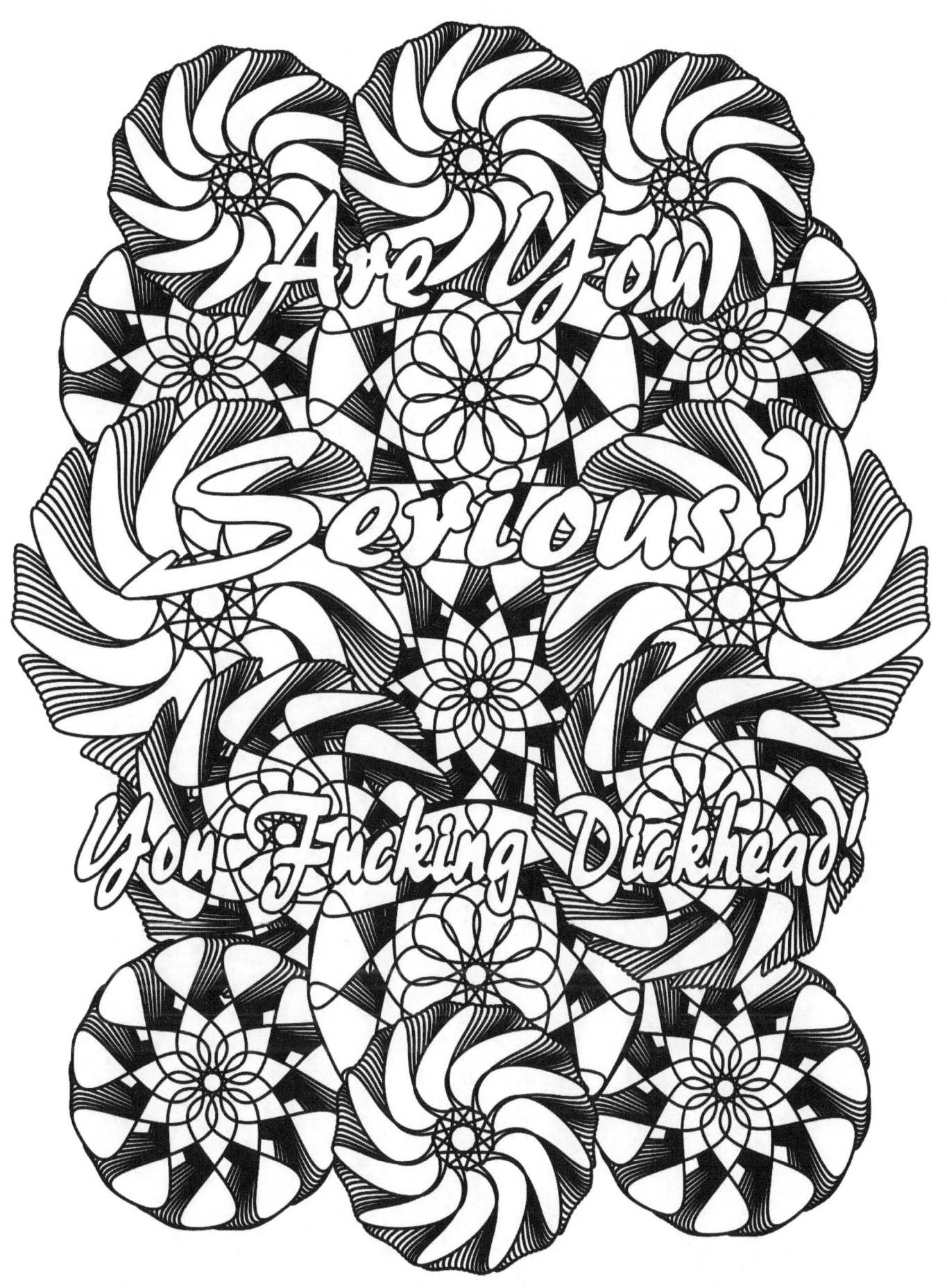

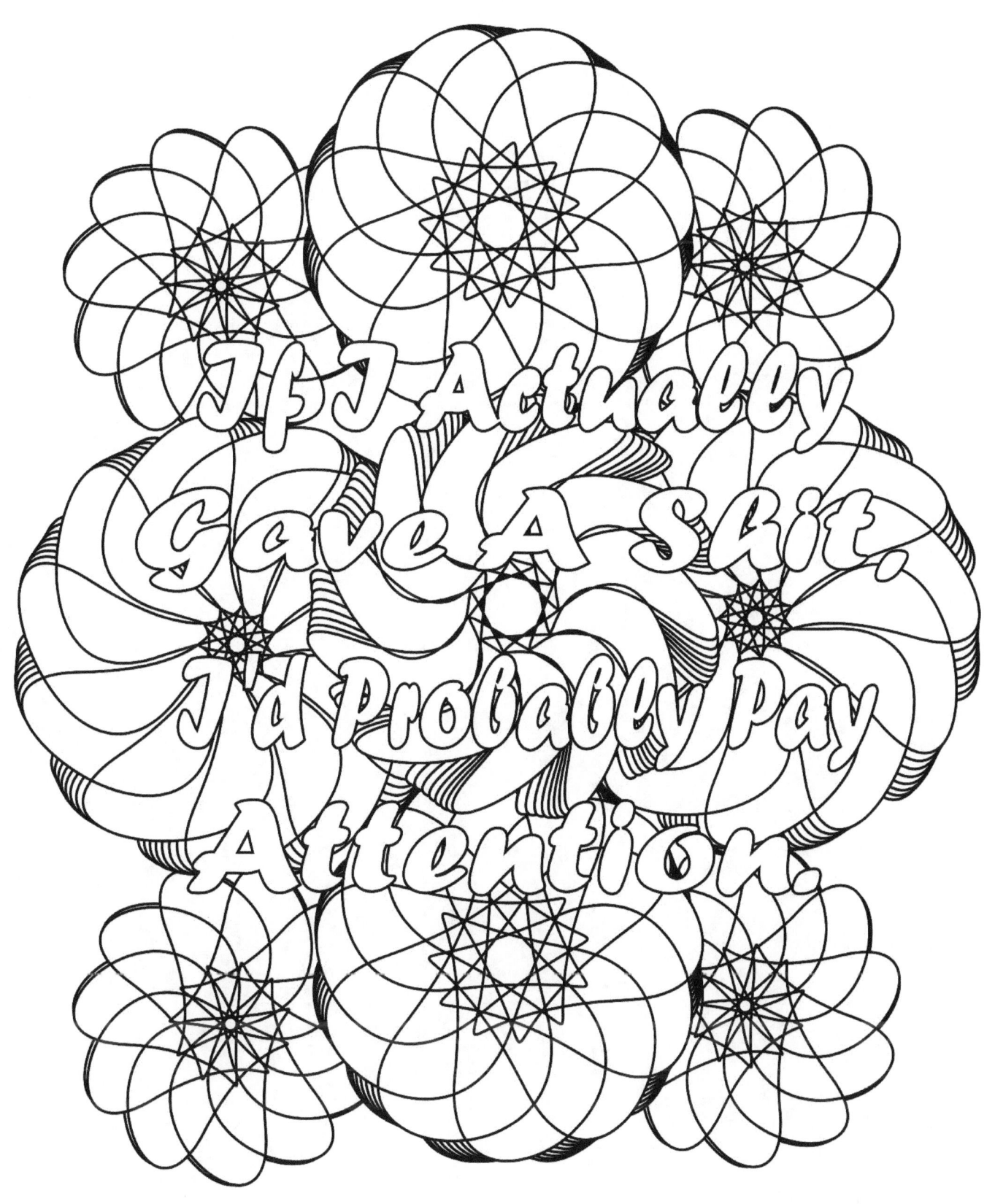

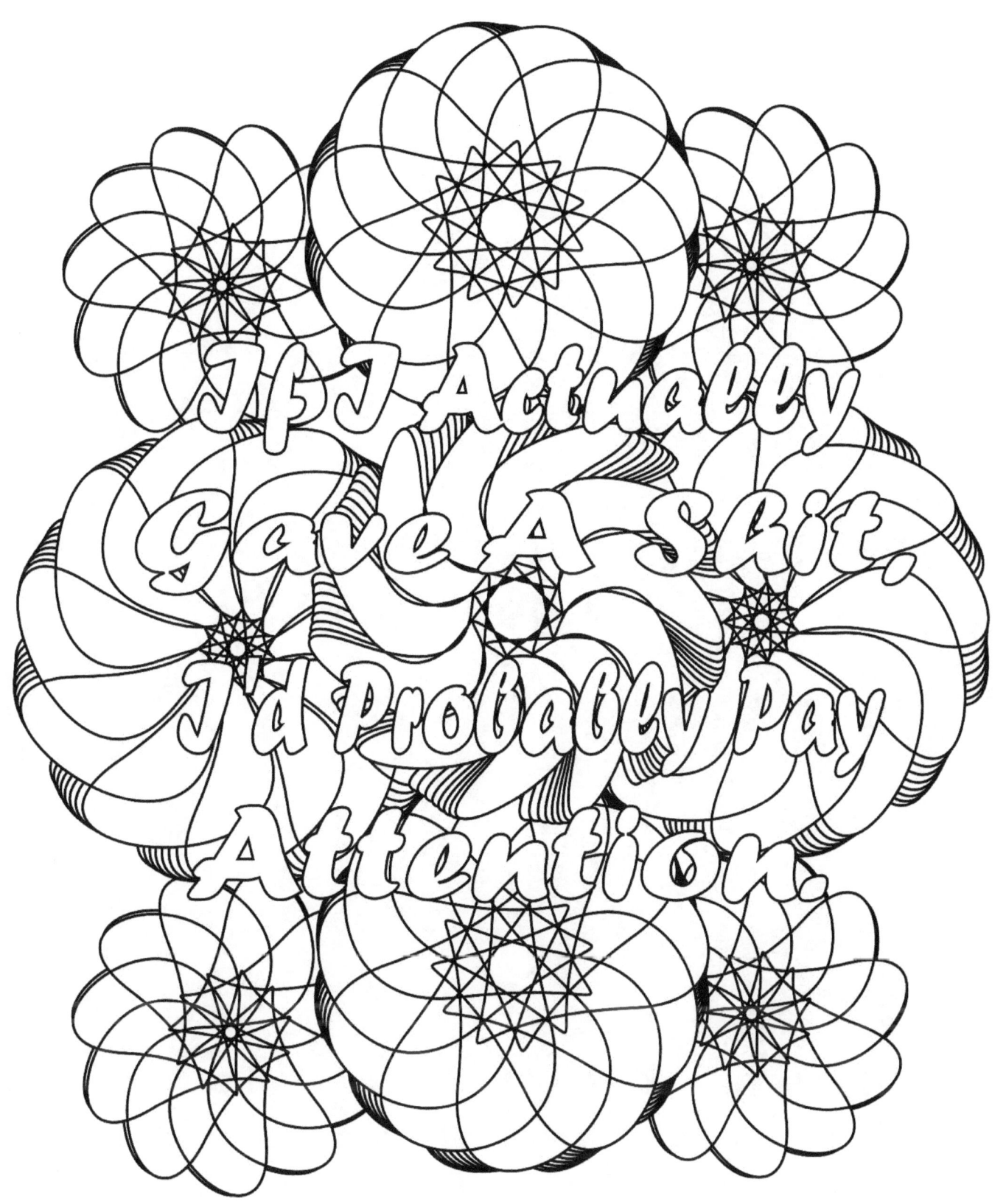

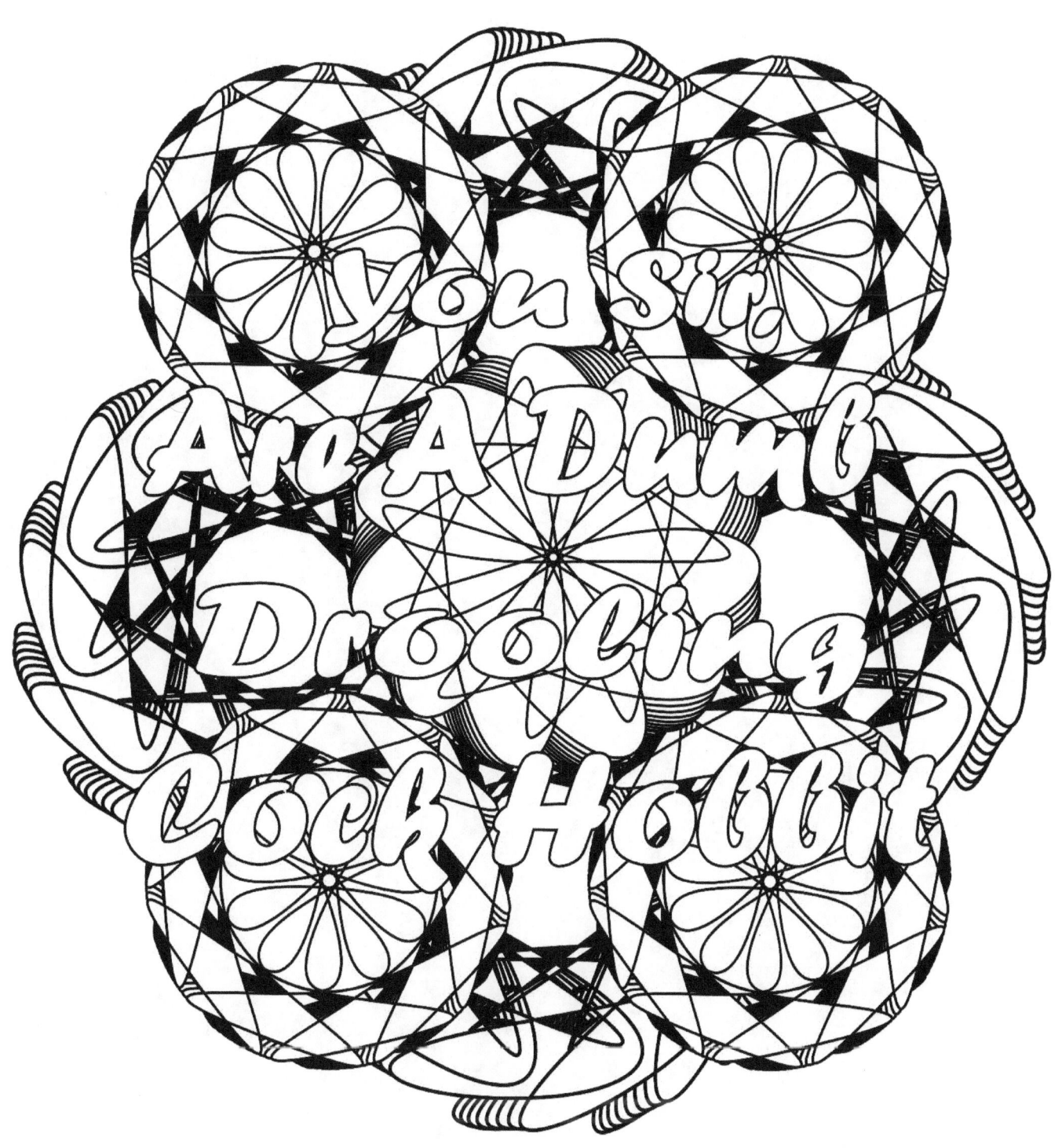

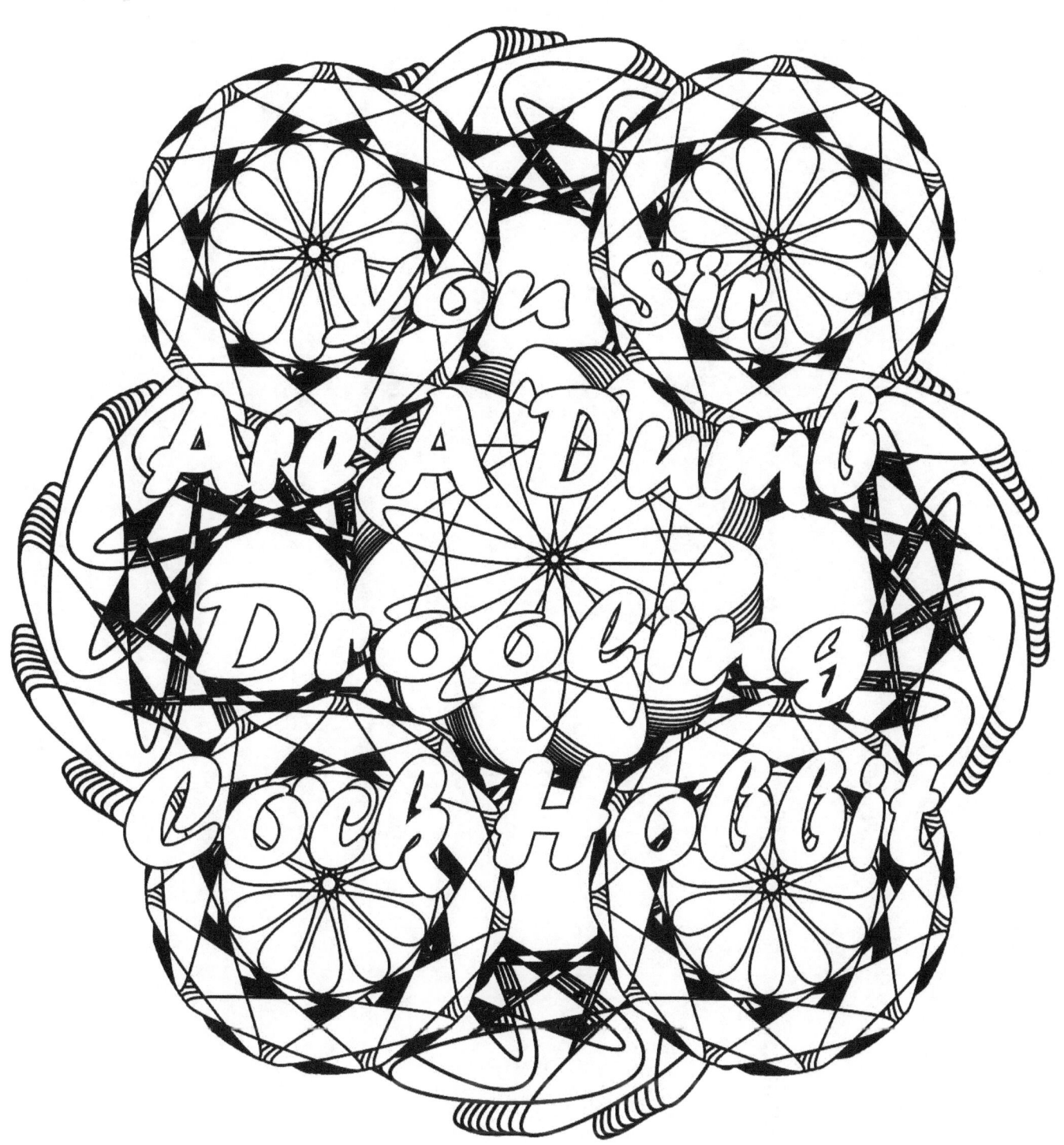

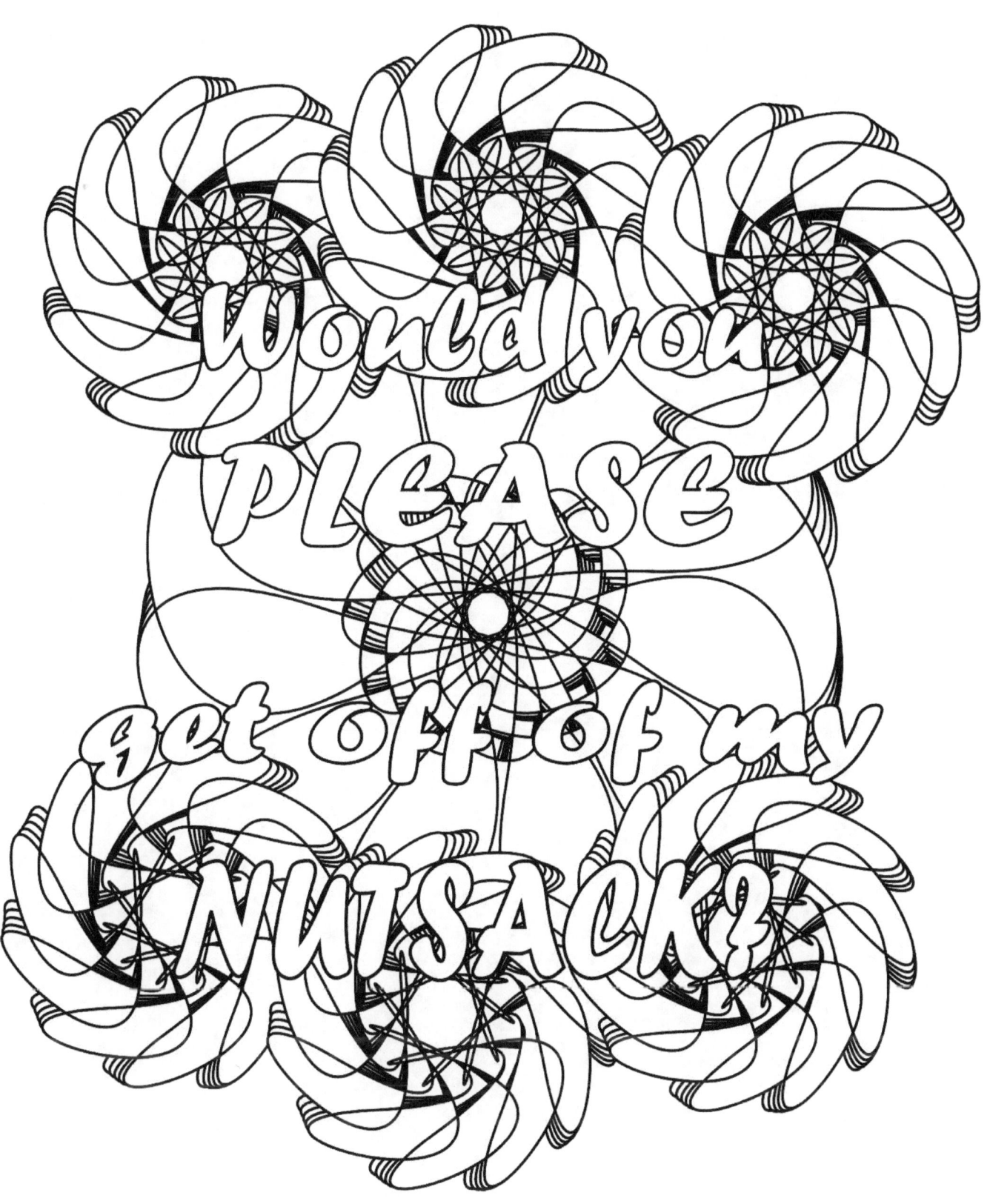

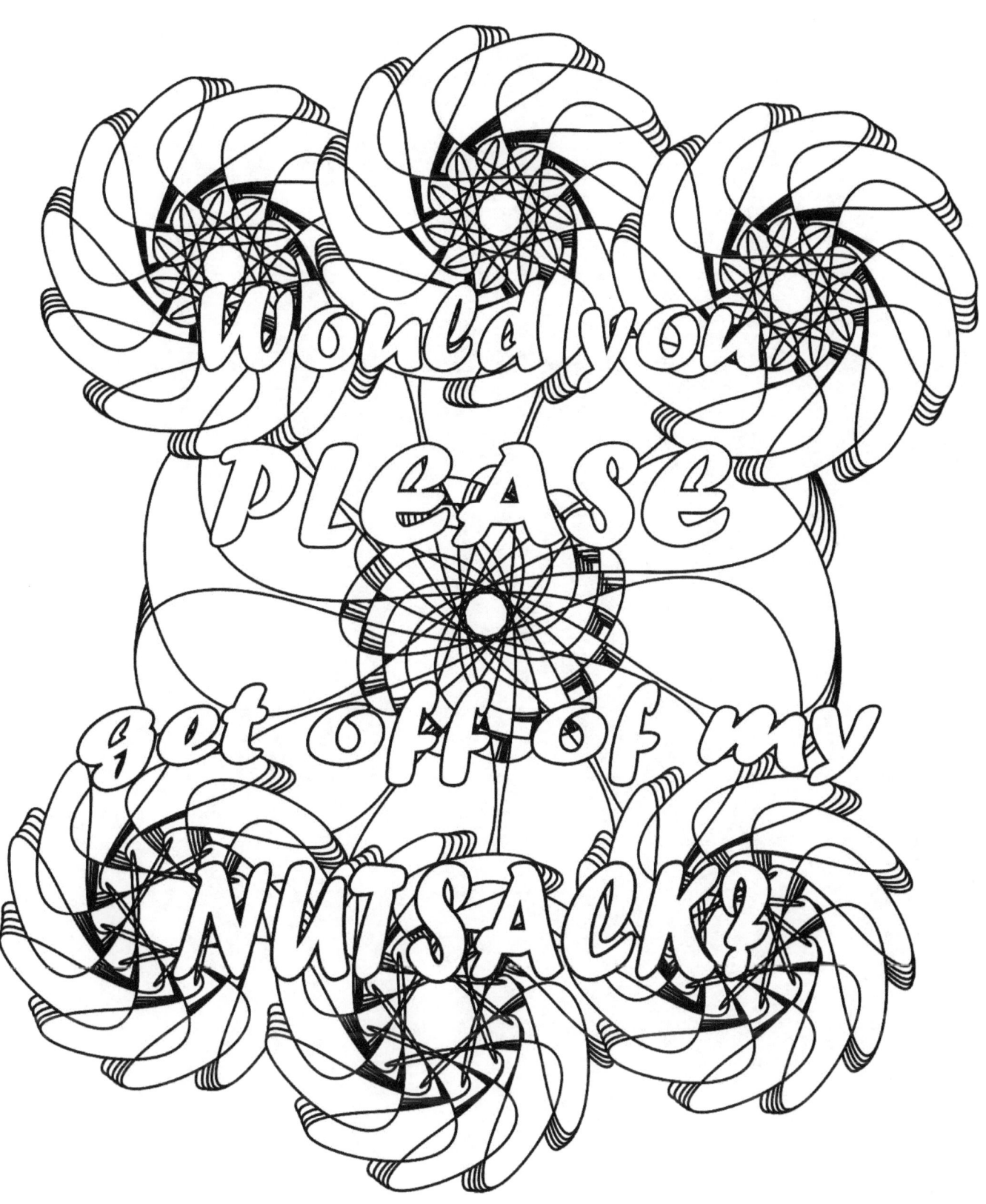

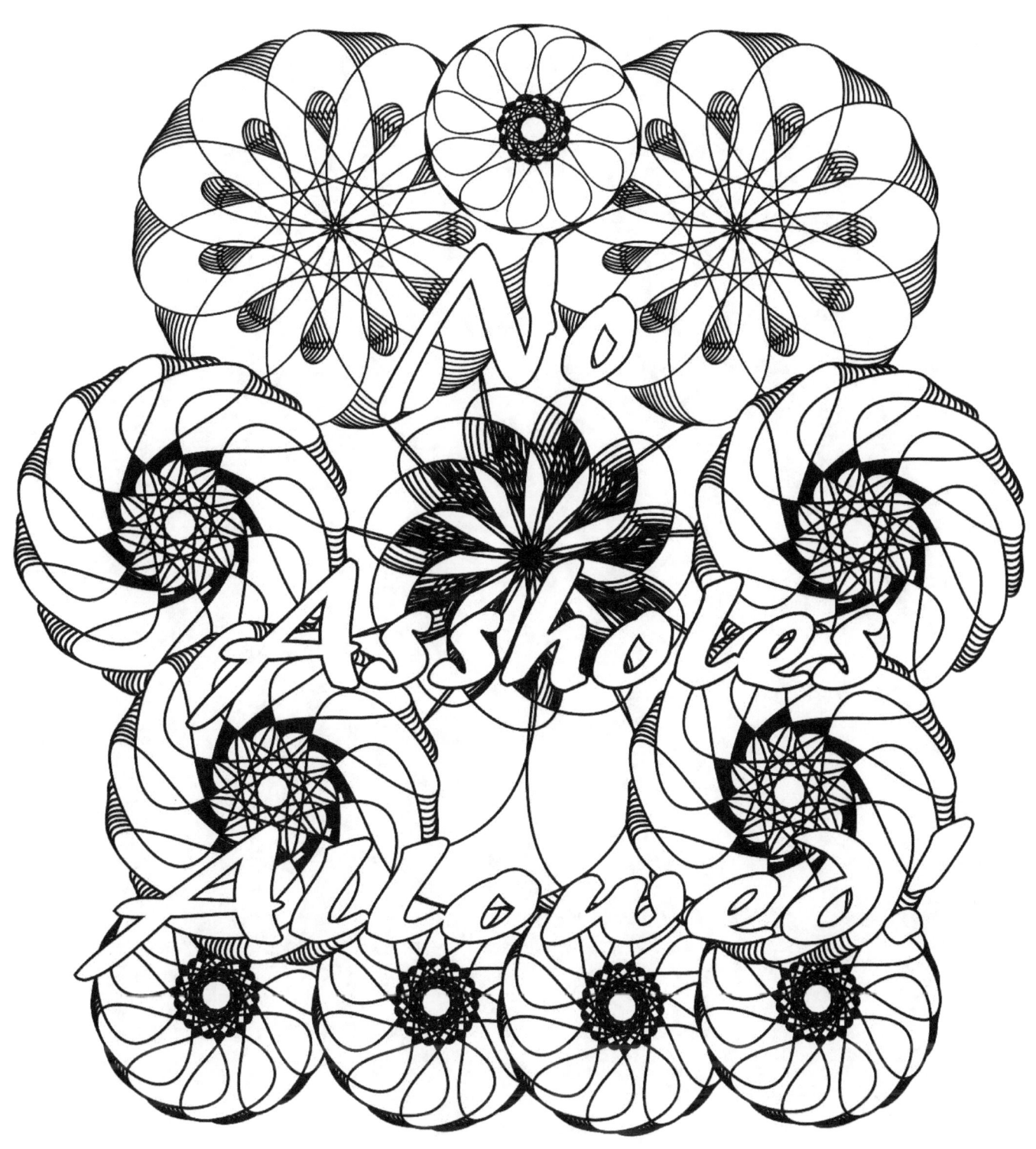

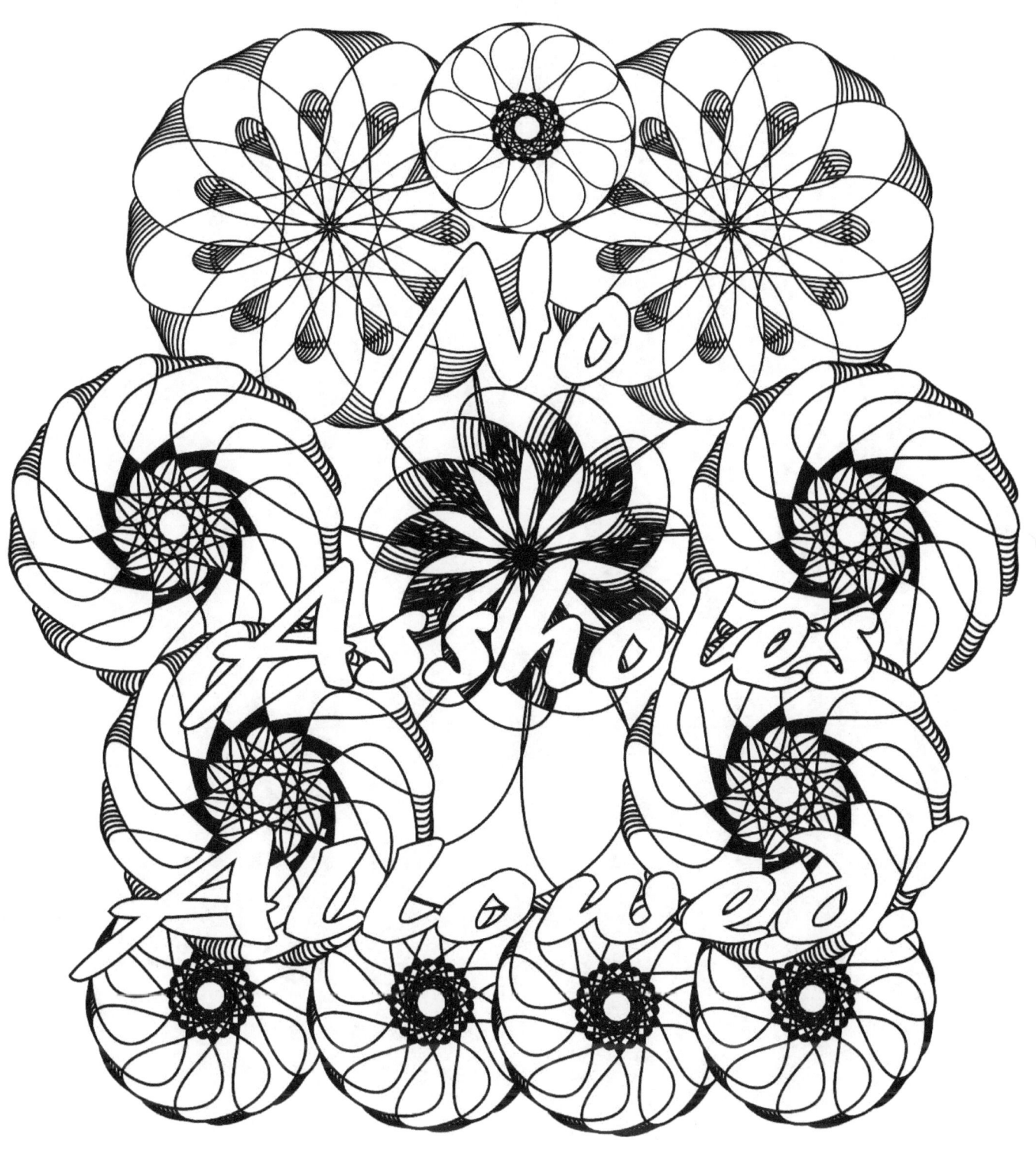

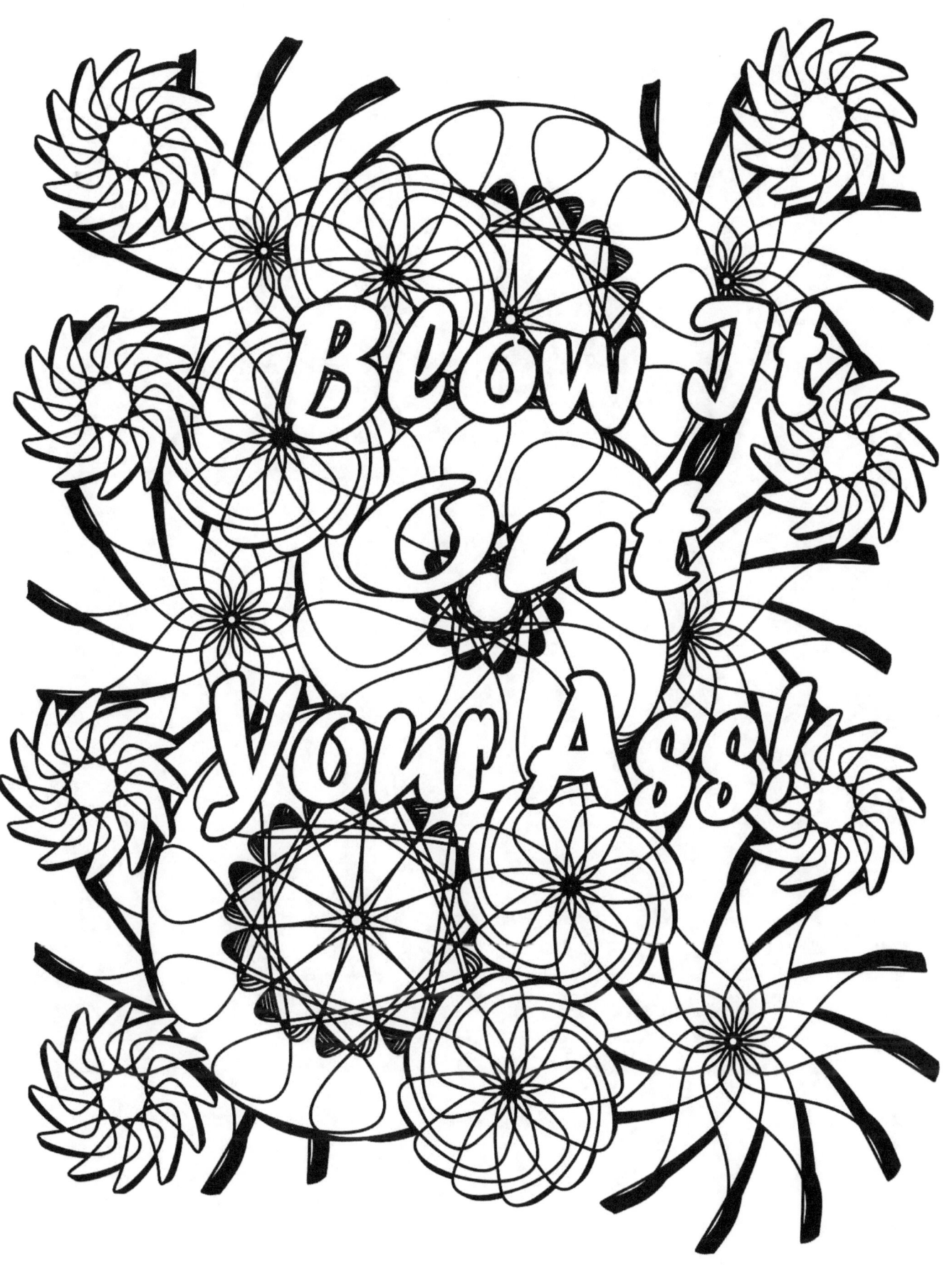

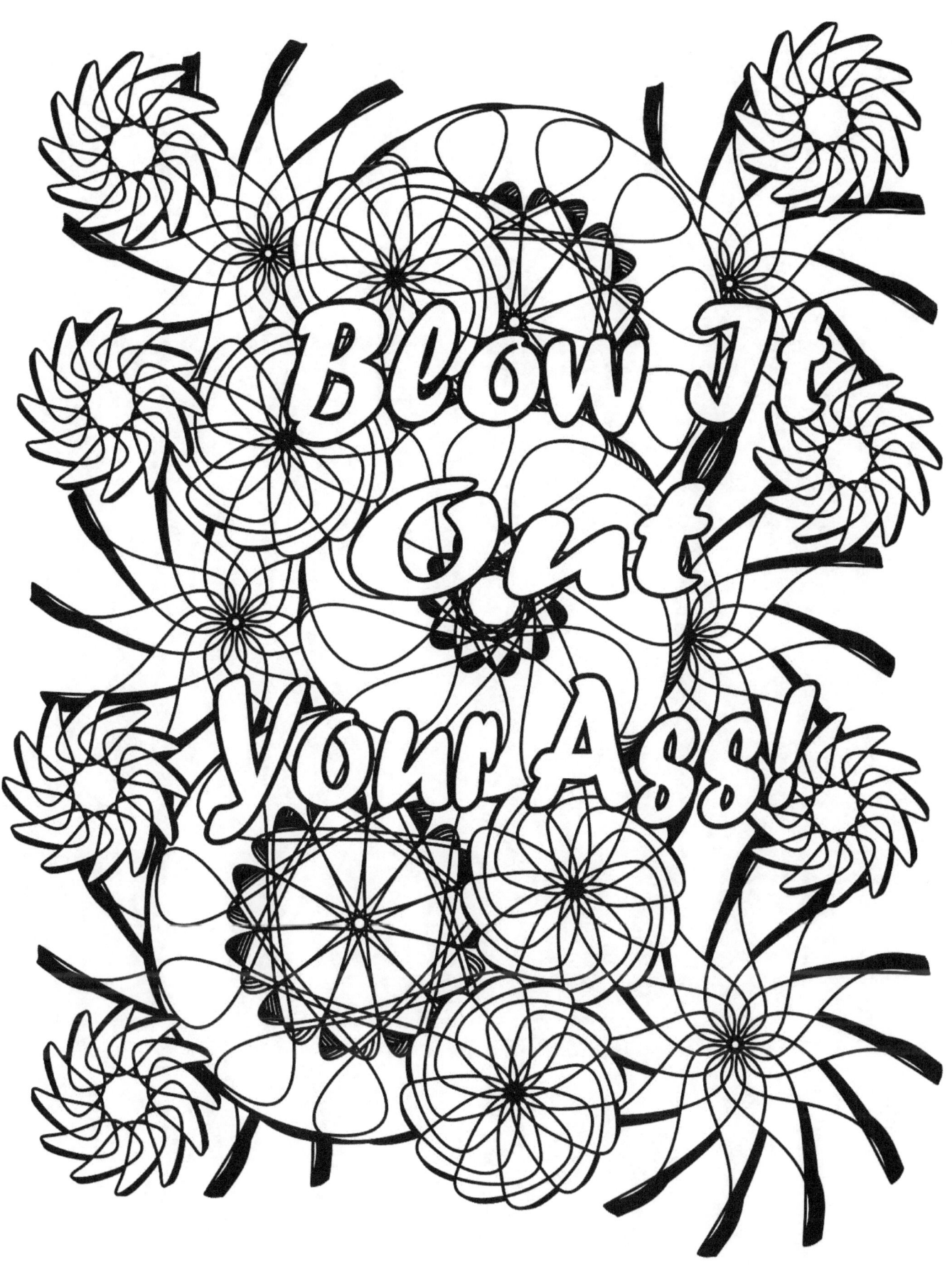

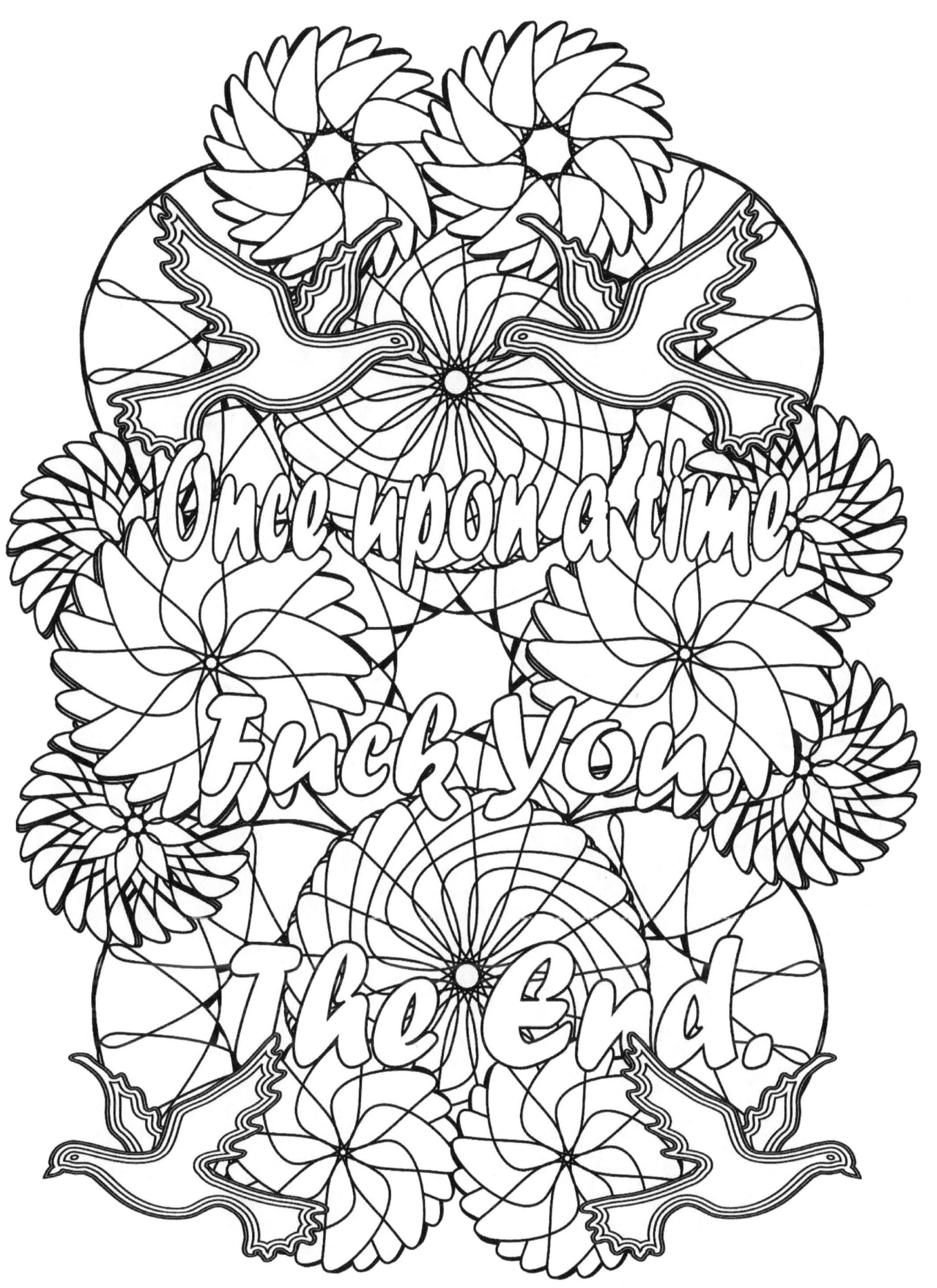

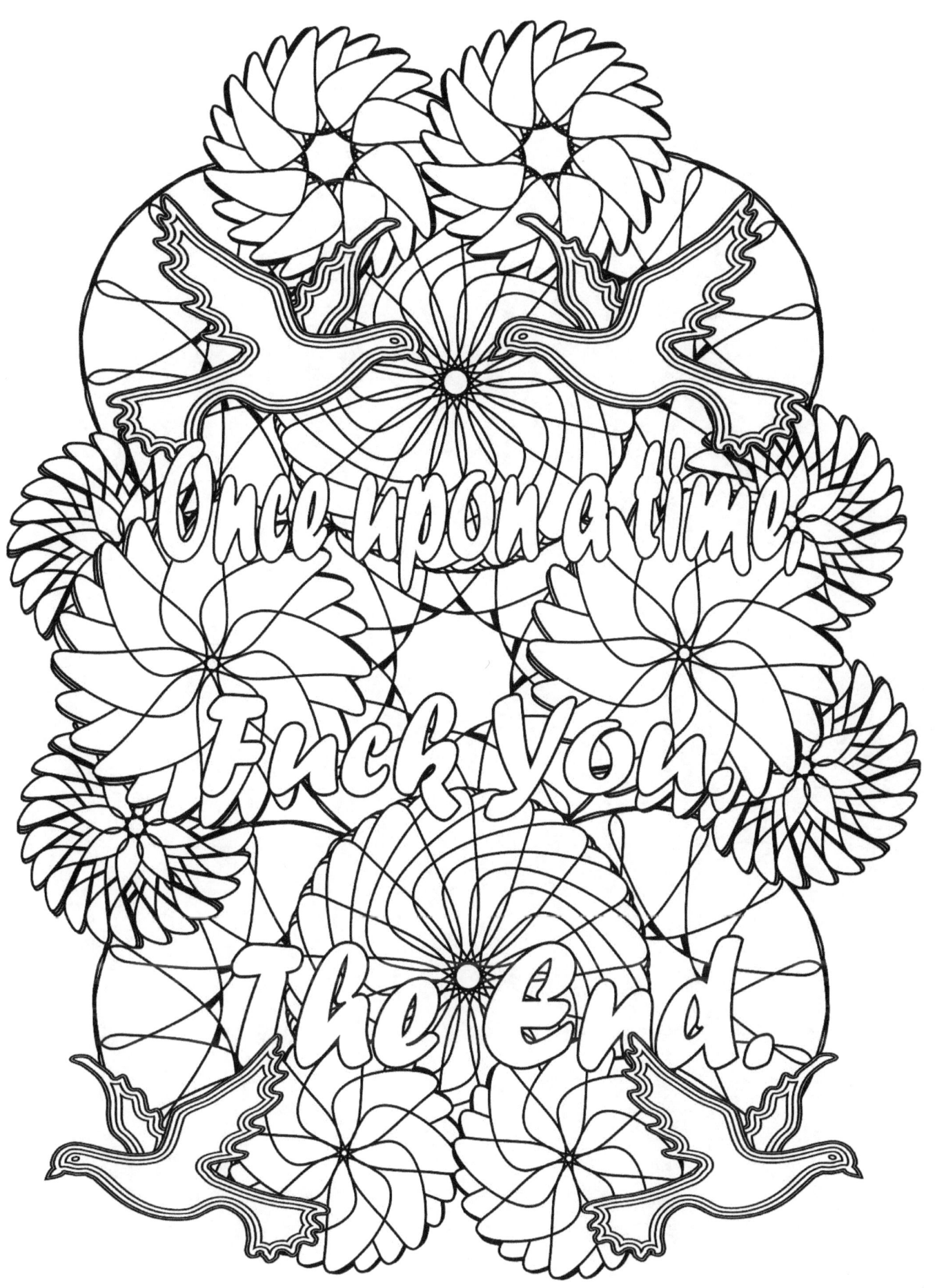